WITHDRAWN
NDSU

HEREDITAS

Seven Essays on the Modern Experience of the Classical

HEREDITAS

SEVEN ESSAYS ON THE MODERN EXPERIENCE OF THE CLASSICAL

EDITED WITH AN INTRODUCTION BY FREDERIC WILL

UNIVERSITY OF TEXAS PRESS, AUSTIN

164456

Library of Congress Card Catalog No. 64–10322
Copyright © 1964 by the University of Texas Press
All Rights Reserved

Manufactured in the United States of America

PN
883
W5

CONTENTS

INTRODUCTION

The persistence of human culture is in itself mysterious and arbitrary. In this it resembles, say, the continuously created universe of some modern theories of cosmology, or that creation which, according to Malebranche, was at every moment maintained in existence by an act of will—of God's will, in that case. That culture should exist is as arbitrary as that we or the universe should be here, which is to say most arbitrary. In both cases the awareness comes rarely. But in both cases the arbitrariness is felt as certain and strong. We *need* not exist; the culture which shapes us and which we shape *need* not exist. These two contingencies have much to do with one another.

Freud made the point forcefully in his later writings that culture is won only at a price, the price of what he sometimes called the rejection or self-denial of instinctual gratification. By this he meant a great deal that has led to controversy and objection. We can now at least rescue, as uncontested Freudian discovery, the idea that a passionate, primitive subconscious, the *id,* must be held back and controlled before the conscious, organizing powers of the mind, the *ego,* can operate to shape a culture. That such exercise of control is precarious, thus that the psychic foundation of the existence of culture is fragile, is proved on every side: by the analysis of dreams, which let the primitive riot at night, or of the vagaries of daily behavior and conversation, which are repeatedly letting culturally objectionable notions slip through; by the analysis of seriously neurotic people, who more than others allow the world to see the turmoil of conflicting suppressed passions under the surface of their behavior; by the analysis of seriously neurotic societies, groups of people who more than others reveal their mass frustrations, in bigotry, orgies, or wars which threaten to nullify the entire social undertaking.

In this perspective a particular tradition *within* culture simply provides a special example of a general situation. Traditions may be specific—religious, literary, philosophical—or more general, identified, for instance, with the productions of an entire nation at a certain time, or over a period of time. In either case a tradition is simply one strand in the tapestry of human culture as a whole. As such it, like the whole of culture, can be maintained in existence only by a continuous process of building: the tradition, like the culture which surrounds it, is forever threatened with disarticulation, collapse. We can sense the arbitrariness of tradition too, at choice, alarming moments.

We sense it often with the classical tradition, that body of artistic, political, philosophical, and religious experience which draws its continuous energy from ancient Greece and Rome. The aesthetic branch, which is of chief interest here, presently arouses our sense of the precariousness of a tradition—and for the paradoxical reason that we are just now, in these years, experiencing a particularly florid outcropping from the living tip of this branch: in architecture classical forms have been revived, and in both a genuine and daring spirit, during the Bauhaus Movement, and in much of Frank Lloyd Wright's work; in painting there is Picasso, as well as a classical mood—generally speaking—in the entire cubist movement; in literature especially there has been a spate of experiments on classical themes—in works by some of the makers of the modern, by Joyce, Yeats, Eliot, Gide, Mann. It is difficult to think of a major twentieth-century writer who has not, in his work, negotiated seriously with the classical. What should be alarming about all this excitement within the tradition?

The answer involves a broad psychological question of no great subtlety but of great impact. As the activity of maintaining and molding the classical aesthetic tradition grows increasingly strenuous, as we see the *tradition being made* on all sides of us, we grow increasingly aware that the tradition *is created,* and thus that it *can be unmade, need* not be made at all. Ours is, I suppose, in some ways like the case of a man who feels he has finally made contact with God; ever after he will realize what extraordinary horizons there are to human experience, and how perilously close the "true" experience is to the mediocrity of existence. Before the realization he didn't know the peril.

It is the intention of the following collection to suggest something of what, in the works of a few contemporaries, constitutes the literary creativity of the classical tradition. No great effort at regimentation has been made in gathering these essays. Those of Part One all put the case for the great present activity and the independent viability of the classical literary tradition. Other ingredients of western culture are not here in question. Classical myth is made to seem self-supporting, when caught up into genuine modern reinterpretations.

Three of the authors deal with whole myths—of Amphitryon, Oedipus, or Odysseus—and with their significant transformation in some contemporary work. What strikes, in each of these cases, is both the infinite fertility of the original legend, and the refinements to which a sensitive author can resubmit it, in interpretation. Mr. Friedman treats *Amphitryon 38* from the standpoint of its contribution to the series of plays on that theme. He shows us the delicious human irreverence of the treatment, where some of the best conversation transpires between Zeus and Alcmena, in a mist of *doubles entendres.* He also leaves us with the impression of compassion, Giraudoux' saving grace; this grace goes out over the deluded Amphitryon when he returns home. Mr. Roudiez, in writing of Robbe-Grillet and Butor, discusses antithetical conceptions of Greek myth, as they are embodied in modern novels. The first makes antimyth, sowing through his novel *Les Gommes* obvious but, as it turns out, completely misleading references to the tale of Oedipus. One assertion of the novel, perhaps the chief, is that myth is meaningless, and that "real life" is in fact denuded of any significance beyond its mere transpiring. Michel Butor, in *L'Emploi du Temps,* looks at the matter through the other end of the telescope. An essential part of his story concerns the subtly introduced parallel between his "hero," M. Revel, and Theseus. Bleston, England, where Revel is staying, in many ways resembles, and in some ways is said to resemble, a labyrinth. And so on. Between Robbe-Grillet and Butor it seems not at all a question of whether to employ myth; simply of whether, and in what sense, meaning should be ascribed to the myth that is used. Kazantzakis presents a much more conventional treatment, in this respect. Like Joyce he is in the epic reinterpretative tradition, though by continuing Homer's *Odyssey* by 33,333 lines he invites comparison even more audaciously. I confine myself to an analysis of his audacious work, with a few concluding observations on its originality.

Mr. Freedman, Mr. Hayman, and Mr. Sullivan move, in that order of specificness, toward a consideration of the detailed linguistic materials in which the classical literary tradition is perpetuated. Mr. Freedman is concerned with Rilke's gods—Apollo, Artemis, Orpheus—and with the intensely personal way in which that poet appropriates this public material to his spiritual uses. Lyric language here bears large mythical weight. Mr. Hayman writes of two aspects of the imagery in *A Portrait of the Artist as a Young Man,* the imagery clusters involved with birds, on the one hand, and labyrinths, on the other. Both entrappedness, at home and in seminary, and desire for flight, pervade the story, and continually emphasize Stephen's plight and possibilities. Mr. Sullivan turns even farther in toward the linguistic process at work in making classical tradition. He studies some of those "outrageous" techniques of deliberate misunderstanding, and half-understanding, by which Pound brought new life into the experience of Propertius. "From an obscure Roman love poet," as Mr. Sullivan says, "popularly estimated as crabbed and difficult, a poet of violent and abrupt transitions, Propertius became, as it were, a modern, and the higher Propertian criticism has not been the same since."

The longest essay, the last one, has gone farthest away from literature in order to consider larger cultural questions. Mr. De Laura asks himself, in terms of T. S. Eliot's changing conceptions of western culture, just what kind of harmony can be established between orthodox Christianity and the pagan classical tradition. This little-asked question is clearly of the greatest urgency to any espouser of the so-called western tradition, with the mixed sources of its values, and the conclusions of the present essay are of great interest; considerable doubt is cast upon the reconcilability of the Christian with the pagan. One comes away knowing that Eliot has been an extremely honest and strenuous struggler with this question. The whole viability of the classical tradition—as well as of the Christian—is here opened to examination.

I have said that the energy of the modern classical tradition, as it exists and is argued in these essays, can alarm with its very message: that such traditions are made by men, that they are immensely valuable, and that they must be maintained minute to minute, like creation in Malebranche's universe. This is of course only one way, and perhaps an unnecessarily dour way, of looking at the matter. But I think this hardly the time in civilization to sit congratulating ourselves on our achievements. Furthermore, there are some real threats, more specific than the "condition humaine."

A complex and mature group of awarenesses is embodied, in the myths and devices of classical literature, which are the product of long experience among the most gifted of people, the ancient Greeks, and their only slightly retrograde followers, the Romans. These awarenesses, unfortunately, are not self-perpetuating, but have been maintained by the guardians of tradition: the schools, the literary creators, the libraries, and at one time the church. The combined efforts of these forces, the general assumption of the value of a "classical education," and the restriction of education to a small minority, who had the leisure for prolonged labor in the niceties of language, all facilitated the maintenance of the tradition prior to this century. Presently, despite the energies to which this collection refers, the tradition has entered some dangerous waters.

Those waters surround the central depths in which the literary workers, referred to here, are swimming profoundly. I refer, and not without some qualms, to the dereliction of the schools and the scholars—not to mention that of the church, in the broadest sense, which is cutting itself off from its traditional sources of strength, without having found new ones. My experience of the schools is limited—to the American system and to a little of England and the European continent. There is unmistakable evidence here, however, that the classical literary tradition has been radically, and critically, cut in half. One half of it has been popularized, so bastardized. In America we are only too aware of this, and I have reason to suspect a little of the same in England. Here in America we find universities teaching the beginnings of Latin to entering students; to students who, for obvious reasons, are too old to savor the routine of learning a difficult ancient language, who have little reason to appreciate the importance of the effort, and who not infrequently groan en masse at the necessity to interrupt football with Latin. Of Greek at this level, the less said the better; few get through the mountains of Xenophon even to the waters of the *Apology*.

Many reasons are adduced for this drying up of the school classical tradition in America. Doubtless they are all true, up to a point. The *myth* of scientific knowledge has taken a toll; the naive conviction that only the experimental method, applied to observable objects, provides true knowledge has temporarily damaged humanitarian studies; but that particular myth is dying. It has been replaced by very different threats. Positivism, with its roots in experimental science, has become rather an independent weapon to wield against imaginative studies, and has most regrettably been wielded by humanitarians, many classicists among them, against their own study. Entirely different threats are posed by "liberal education," especially that cramped form of Deweyism which finds its way into the schools of education dominant in so many American state universities. From this direction comes discouragement of hard study, the immediate practical benefits of which are not evident. It would only be honest to add, among these threats, the immense task of educating millions of young people, and the great number of important subjects which it is even urgently relevant for such people to have touched, in order to respond to the world around them.

Assessment of these inner threats to the tradition is sobering, and warrant for a dour mood in the midst of celebration. Warrant too for a particular sense of the burden lying on the creators, the literary men whose making of a classical renaissance in this century has been so encouraging. Those men have done much, not of course out of any sense of mutual, concerted effort, but, what is far more important, out of totally independent realizations of *how* it is still possible to make important literary statements. I don't imply, for a moment, that the re-experience of classical themes has been central in the work of any of the major literary figures of this century. I do mean, though, that such re-experience has touched many of them deeply, becoming the motive of characteristic and searching expressions.

I now only wish those expressions were more widely read and experienced, and created for broader consumption. Shelley spoke of poets as "unacknowledged legislators of the world." Schiller had earlier argued, in his *Aesthetic Education of Mankind,* the social force of such legislation. There, as a young man, he had sized up the implications of what he viewed as the death of Christianity. He remarked on the power of drama to substitute for religion, especially on the part played by Attic drama in the education of the Greek people through enjoyment. It struck him that society had no more effective means of educating—i.e., civilizing—its members than through drama, or other forms of art; no better way of preserving its character as culture.

It would be more than naive, today, to expect such large-scale power to be exercised by any form of art which did not recommend itself to the mass media: to TV, the movies, or at least the newspapers. And of no serious contemporary literary art can this be said. We get no closer to it, I suppose, than the rather self-conscious epic and popular drama of Brecht. Williams and Miller, in America, or the whimsical creators of *théâtre de l'absurde,* on the Continent, offer little prospect of becoming effective cultural forces. Does not the mythical power inherent in the themes of classical literature, even as we have seen it released in certain contemporary retreatments, promise such force? I think so. Clearly we cannot turn to the makers of modern liteature with suggestions that they pick up these themes even more systematically, making poems, dramas, and novels which will realize the inherent and broad shaping powers of ancient myth. Literature—especially of that sort—is not created by fiat. And in any case those writers could reply that it was *they* who gave *us* the idea of making the suggestion. But we can certainly point to what they have done, and to its general significance; and we are free to hope that the broadest interests of the tradition, of the culture which carries it, and of the men who write for it can correctly be seen as one. For only in that way will culture continue to have the chance of self-creation.

F. W.

Austin, Texas

PART ONE

The Classical in Modern Literature

GODS, HEROES, AND RILKE

By Ralph Freedman

To PLACE as evanescent a poet as Rainer Maria Rilke in the company of heroes and gods may appear cruelly ironic. But actually Rilke's way of using ancient gods and heroes in his late poetry expresses a pattern which had developed in German literature since the eighteenth century. After the early romantic writers had rejected the "classicism" of Goethe and Schiller, those ancient gods who survived underwent a strange metamorphosis. Schiller had still been able to celebrate the gods of Greece, believing he had evoked a true image of antiquity. Even Hölderlin, seeking to recapture the ideal Schiller had charted, praised in his *Hymns* a world dominated by the ancient deities. But Hölderlin also created a modern Hyperion who failed to fulfill the ideal of ancient Greece. When all is lost, instead of dying the death of Thermopylae, this new Hyperion sings a hymn to the Soul. The classical hero became no longer the model for form which had survived in the great Greek statues. Nor was he, in the end, the guide for action, as Homer and Virgil had presented him. Under the impact of nineteenth-century metaphysics the outlines of the Greek hero were blurred by nineteenth-century conceptions of the self.

The gesture of philosophizing a familiar image is deeply linked with a mode in nineteenth-century criticism and poetry, and with post-Kantian thought. The hero as a transcendental image of the self, combining the inner and the outer, feeling and thought, became inevitably fused with the traditional concept of ancient gods as representatives of man's ultimate ambition. Even Nietzsche's Apollo and Dionysus were after all only labels for ideas of order and passion expressed in tragedy. In our own time this notion of the hero appears even more sharply. Sartre's Zeus and Camus's Sisyphus, like Rilke's Apollo and Orpheus, are qualities defining modes of existence. As Erich Heller made clear in *The Disinherited Mind,* they exist "by virtue of that peculiar adjustment to more modern attitudes of the soul which was forced upon Greek mythology by the spiritual need and hunger of modernity." [1]

Clearly, then, my title is considerably less ironic than it appears on the surface. In all of Rilke's work, verse and prose appeal to us through images of the heroic and the divine. His early poems offer few allusions to classical figures. Tender souls, monks, virgins at the moment of ripening convey a feeling for a reality beneath gross appearances. But while these figures continue to be most important even in his later work, controlling roles are assumed more and more by Old Testament prophets, angels, and Greek heroes and gods. Their importance increases as Rilke develops an awareness of their significance to himself. In the spirit of Novalis he came to see the hero as an embodiment of his inner life, as the material through which he could manifest the creative act.

A glance at Rilke's life makes clear that his personal heroes had always been artists. Nietzsche, both as philosopher and poet, supplied him with his first sense of direction as a young man and maintained a significant hold upon his imagination throughout his life. After Rilke's

[1] *The Disinherited Mind* (New York: Farrar, Straus, and Cudahy, 1957), p. 131.

journey to Russia, Tolstoy became for him an overwhelming figure, for he saw in the Russian master a kind of dialectical union of the towering hero and the idea of humility, a dichotomy which he experienced within himself. But most important for his *technique* was the French sculptor Rodin, whom he served as a disciple from 1902 on and as a secretary in 1905–1906. Although Rodin himself was often uncomfortable with his German admirer, he remained for Rilke the artist-hero par excellence. Not only did Rilke explain Rodin as an artist in two brilliant essays (1903 and 1907); he also made him the master of his poetic vision and method.

The nature of the self is most maturely explored in three collections of poems which round out Rilke's career, *New Poems* (1906–1908), the *Duino Elegies* (1912–1922), and the *Sonnets to Orpheus* (1922–1923). In each of these collections, but particularly in the first and the last, heroes of antiquity explain and represent the creative act. They appear as stylized portraits of the artist-hero—the towering or central vision— evolving from a plastic to a metaphysical image.

II

The poems written mostly in Paris between 1903 and 1908 (*New Poems*) are new poems indeed. Not only do they replace the evocation of feelings with the depiction of objects and scenes, but they also reflect a new vision of the self and its relationship to the world. In the conclusion of his second essay, Rilke wrote about Rodin:

His things could not wait; they had to be accomplished. He had long since foreseen their homelessness. Only one choice remained: to throttle them within him or to win that heaven for them which is beyond the mountain. And that was his task. In a gigantic arc he has raised the world above us and has placed it into nature.[2]

The statement signifies a new experience which goes beyond the preoccupation with objective poetry usual since the French symbolists.

[2] *Gesammelte Werke* (Leipzig: Inselverlag, 1930), IV, 418.

It is even more than an attempt to depict vital experience through an intense concentration on objects with which we have been familiar since Hulme, Pound, and the imagists. It injects a highly specialized idea into poetic technique, opening poetry to a new dimension.

Although Rilke had always been interested in the relationship between poetry, painting, and sculpture—a passion he shared with Baudelaire and many of his own *fin de siècle* contemporaries—it is through Rodin that he saw this relationship as peculiarly apposite to the concept of the self. The body had not been heretofore an identity. In the Rodin essay, however, Rilke gives it an almost metaphysical status. Rodin, he wrote, "created bodies which touched and cohered in every part like interlocked struggling beasts that fall like a thing into a depth." [3] It is thus a statue, immobile and yet in motion, in which each hand or arm is an organism itself, but recreated by the total body as a whole. In this way the human form also mirrors the universal form of nature, which likewise unifies independently existing things, as for Novalis each artist mirrors God's creation and contemplation of the world.

The sculptures, paintings, and other images in *New Poems* reflect such an "organic" union and disparity between the body, representing the self, and the world of things he includes. But it must be evident that the independent things he confronts are not the ordinary perceptions with which we are familiar from epistemology. Inanimate objects in a state of nature or of art—animals, human figures, even trees, houses, bridges, or fields—exist in the same way as Rodin's hands and arms. They are, then, not sensations formed by a perceiving mind. Rather, they are components of an entire universe.

In their "homeless" state things oppress the artist. By this Rilke means that if the poet is incapable of providing things with a "refuge" or

[3] *Ibid.,* p. 336. Translation cited from Geoffrey H. Hartman, *The Unmediated Vision* (New Haven: Yale University Press, 1954), p. 78. Hartman's chapter includes a more extensive discussion of these points.

"home" of organic form, he experiences himself as being assailed by them, as St. Anthony is assailed by temptations. Such an action of things on a mind is brilliantly illustrated in some of the images in Rilke's poetic novel, *The Notebooks of Malte Laurids Brigge* (1914). Here a sensitive young Dane in Paris imagines himself constantly subjected by the action of things. His agitated mind, for example, feels streetcars running over his prostrate body, ringing wildly. In a memory of childhood he recalls how in the heightened vision of fever a button on his bedclothes grew larger than his head, threatening to overwhelm him. The sewage pipe on the remaining wall of a demolished house creeps towards him like a snake. But actually these things are moved by rhythms and forms which the artist must recognize, whose occult meaning he must fathom. In *New Poems* the purpose of representation is to externalize such a form in particular bodies and scenes. Then things could cease to be "homeless" because they would be part of a figure which also represents the poet, the self. A controlling force would be implicit, or immanent, in their form.

It is not surprising in this perspective that each of the two series of *New Poems* begins with a poem on Apollo. In both "Early Apollo" and "The Torso of an Archaic Apollo" the hero is a plastic image, a work of sculpture. In "Early Apollo" the figure is still pure form. Its ordering force has not yet been obscured by the world of things seeking their home. It is pure light, too bright to be borne by the unprotected eye. The hero is not only pristine and undefiled, but as yet unengaged in the world of things.

> Wie manches Mal durch das noch unbelaubte
> Gezweig ein Morgen durchsieht, der schon ganz
> im Frühling ist: so ist in seinem Haupte
> nichts, was verhindern könnte, dass der Glanz
>
> aller Gedichte uns fast tödlich träfe;
> denn noch kein Schatten ist in seinem Schaun,

zu kühl für Lorbeer sind noch seine Schläfe
und später erst wird aus den Augenbrau'n
hochstämmig sich der Rosengarten heben,
aus welchem Blätter, einzeln, ausgelöst
hintreiben werden auf des Mundes Beben,

der jetzt noch still ist, niegebraucht und blinkend
und nur mit seinem Lächeln etwas trinkend
als würde ihm sein Singen eingeflösst.

Apollo, then, is a center of light: the sun at dawn in early spring before foliage obscures its glare. Like Rilke's virginal girls on the brink of maturity, he is as yet "unused." Unlike the original Greek god, this Apollo is sublimely passive. "[There] is nothing *in* his head that could prevent that the glow/ of all poems strike us nearly fatally" runs a literal transcription of the line between the first and second quatrains. This sentence not only links up unambiguously the static form with the deadly fire of the poetic imagination, it also establishes a relationship between the latent power within the luminous head and the profuse manifold it must inevitably confront. The world of things which will emerge from his brow—the rose garden and petals—will be ordered from within. The sculptured hero's *passivity* is essential to the poem. The things, which will burgeon from his brow, will shower their petals over him. Moreover, a theme of absence is sounded: Apollo's forming of the world of things is placed in the *future*.

The poem elaborates the contrast between the concentrated light in Apollo's features and the manifold of nature he will suffer and eventually form. The first is rigorous and statuesque. The latter is latent in him, projected into a soft motion, scattered, discrete. In obscuring his glance they also *will* furnish the motion and sound that will turn the light of the formal Apollo into the poet's song. For it is the song, as yet unsung, that will be the form of art in which the passive Apollo will be caught—the rose petals floating "on his mouth's quivering." The image is released from its spatial shape and transformed into action. The motion of the petals, always seen in the future, creates a projected *event,* through which they are turned into a song. Drifting leaves, a waiting mouth, the image of drink, and the idea of a song not emitted but infused—these form an oddly inverse chain through which the plastic form is changed into a poem.

The concluding image of the quivering mouth is of no small significance to Rilke's conception of Apollo. For here, as elsewhere in Rilke, the mouth is made into the unwilling poet's instrument of torment, precisely because it is the instrument of his song. In his poem on Jeremiah in *New Poems, II,* the prophet berates God.

> Welchen Mund hast du mir zugemutet,
> damals, da ich fast ein Knabe war:
> eine Wunde wurde er: nun blutet
> aus ihm Unglücksjahr um Unglücksjahr.

The key to this stanza is the enormous passivity attributed even to the fiery biblical prophet. The mouth was given him, forced on him. It is an open wound from which bleed the unfortunate years. In the same way, the mouth of Apollo is waiting: its expectant tremor is open to the infusion of his song. At this point, the resemblance between Apollo and Rilke's virginal women has become inescapable. Their awakening, too, is always in the future: their fulfillment, like that of Apollo, is vouchsafed by its absence. To be wholly a lyrical self the image of Apollo must in the end be fertilized by a song created by the radiance of things within an illuminating form.

This way of seeing the figure of beauty is quite different even from similar forms created by French poets from whom Rilke undoubtedly borrowed. For example, the "Early Apollo" inevitably calls to mind Baudelaire's "La Beauté," with which it shares the use of the statue. Baudelaire's figure is a "dream of stone," acting through its cold and detached beauty, as the poets are smashed against her indifferent breast. They are not identified with the image of beauty, although they foolishly pine for it, nor do they become its mouth of singing. Rather, they are compulsive lovers unreasonably drawn to their certain fate, while the body's translucent light remains in the well-ordered lines and in the eternal mirrors of the eyes. But for Rilke, who seeks to escape the Baudelairean dualism, poet and image cannot remain separate. Their unity is rendered by an organic form, line become event, or action, an animated mouth, petals growing from brows and showering back upon them, a cycle, a waiting, which, almost on the brink of fulfillment, the poet will render in his song.

As we turn to the second series of *New Poems* we encounter a different Apollo. It is not the Greek god himself—the early poem bore no relation to him either—but its *torso*. The luminosity which had shone forth from the god's head in the first poem is now seen in a headless form. The light, or ordering force, which had been latent in the early Apollo's head is now suffused throughout the body.

Archäischer Torso Apollos

Wir kannten nicht sein unerhörtes Haupt,
darin die Augenäpfel reiften. Aber
sein Torso glüht noch wie ein Kandelaber,
in dem sein Schauen, nur zurückgeschraubt,

sich hält und glänzt. Sonst könnte nicht der Bug
der Brust dich blenden, und im leisen Drehen
der Lenden könnte nicht ein Lächeln gehen
zu jener Mitte, die die Zeugung trug.

Sonst stünde dieser Stein entstellt und kurz
unter der Schultern durchsichtigem Sturz
und flimmerte nicht so wie Raubtierfelle;

und bräche nicht aus allen seinen Rändern
aus wie ein Stern: denn da ist keine Stelle,
die dich nicht sieht. Du musst dein Leben ändern.

If "Early Apollo" evokes its promise through the future tense, the predominant mood in the "Torso" is the *subjunctive*. This tentative mode is made possible by the idea of absence, which is made into an ideal *presence.* No actual Apollonian head could have ever been as perfect as the source of light the shining torso suggests. True to Rilke's conception of Rodin, the fragmentary body is also a living form in and for itself. Its shape, "bursting" with light, speaks to us in all its perspectives. Yet the lingering light, like a candelabrum turned down and dimmed, had its ultimate source in the absent head. Its ordering force acts through its *absence.*

The entire poem creates its imperious command—*You must change your life*—through negation. The very first line is a compilation of negatives. "Wir kannten *nicht* sein unerhörtes Haupt." The first negative, of course, is *not:* we did *not* know his head. *Unerhört* gives us a second negative. The pertinent dimensions of this world are "unheard of," familiar in our own idiom, and "unheard" in the sense of "not listened to," as a prayer is not properly heard by God. The absent, unknown head, then, is "not heard" (or not perceived) and "unheard of"—both stark negatives. Yet these negatives are linked to a strongly positive noun, *Haupt.* Although this word, which is also used in "Early Apollo," is perfectly conventional poetic German for "head," it also carries with it a meaning of "capital" or "chief." This connotation significantly describes the head's function in both poems: the expectant center of illumination in the first, the unheard-of, unperceived source of light in the second. Moreover, in the "Torso," as in "Early Apollo," the head is a source of growth. The future rose gardens that will spring from Apollo's brow have become eyes' apples (in German, an acceptable idiomatic term for "eyeballs") which had once ripened in now absent sockets.

The use of negation to achieve a concentration of the image leads to a tighter form and syntax than in the earlier poem. Whereas "Early Apollo" progressed through an intensifying use of the copula *and,* through which we ascend from pure light to the falling petals of rose gardens, in the "Torso" everything depends on the pivotal word *else* (*sonst*). In both the second and the third stanzas this word controls the poem as a whole, gathering all its images into a single unit. Instead of culminating a linear progression in the image of the mouth, which provides the reversal in "Early Apollo," this poem reaches its peak in the center, with the image suggested by the absent genitals. In this way, the faint sexual allusion to the mouth in "Early Apollo" is now magnified by a direct, if negative sexual reference: the center of torso and poem alike is the place which "bore procreation." This "center" is not expectant, as in the earlier poem, but absent, removed. The form is objectified by having created the appropriate line through the absent organ. For this reason, the concluding tercet can deal with the problem of content and form more successfully. The nonexistent source of illumination irradiates the form, making it glisten like the pelts of beasts of prey. Yet motion must follow, if the poem is to be a song as well as a description. Gingerly, always in the subjunctive, the sculptured form is dissolved:

> und bräche nicht aus allen seinen Rändern
> aus wie ein Stern . . .

Overflowing its spatial mold, the figure maintains its unity at the same time as it expands. Seeing its onlooker from all perspectives (like the objects viewing the poet in Baudelaire's "Correspondances"), the form elicits the exhortation: *You must change your life.* The absence, yet the pervasiveness, of the ordering force has created a meaning which demands of poet and reader a new mode of experience. The sudden, unexpected breaking of the aesthetic illusion through which we find ourselves transported from an externalized, spatial situation into one involving ourselves as persons recalls Baudelaire's exhortation to the reader in "Au Lecteur": "Hypocrite reader, you, my twin, my brother." It unites poet and reader, drawing them together into the poem's statement. In Rilke's poem the self, manifested by the truncated Apollo, is a luminous image, overflowing from within through the symmetry of its shape.

Similar examples could be drawn from both series of *New Poems*. As Rilke followed Rodin's advice to visit the cages in the Jardin des Plantes and to observe objects and people in the Luxembourg Gardens, he became more and more fascinated by the new mode of objective presentation. For he discovered that he could write poems which do not merely borrow painters' subjects, or reproduce their work, but which use the identical techniques. He saw objects in a different light, formed by their absences, by negative space. But he also saw them in relation to his philosophical purpose: to seek a true representation of the self through the creative act, a hero who would include—and here technique merges with Rilke's mystical ideas—the visible and the invisible, movement and stasis. These relations varied in different poems. In his famous poem "Der Panther," for example, he briefly projected himself into the dim consciousness of the large pacing cat. As through the half-drawn shutter of its eyes an image falls, then moves to the heart and dies, we note the obverse of the sort of perception attributed to Apollo. The circumscribed pacing continues to eternity. No luminosity radiates outward from the center. This kind of negation does not culminate in a formal experience.

New Poems, then, attempts to render spatially the artist's comprehension of his world, to reproduce in words Rodin's conception of bodies. But it might be appropriate to reiterate at this point that painting had always been important for Rilke as a further dimension of poetic technique; not only Rodin but also Cézanne had been extremely important to him as a poet. During 1901 and 1902 he had stayed at the artists' colony at Worpswede near Bremen, where he had been intimate with painters like Otto Modersohn and Paula Modersohn-Becker and where his wife, Clara Westhoff, had also been a resident. But, beyond personal relations, he concerned himself diligently with the significance of spatial form to poetic technique. His *Book of Images,* or, more properly, of *Pictures,* contains a multitude of pictorial vignettes, such as "Der Ritter." But it was through Rodin, and, finally, through his reading of French Parnassian and symbolist poetry, that he arrived at a union of his technical interest with his philosophical rationale.

The unifying force, or luminosity, which Rilke identified with Apollo, entails also an ideological position that prevailed in the French literary climate of the turn of the century in which Rilke lived. Unusually sensitive and open to influence, he literally sucked in the atmosphere provided by the symbolist movement and its followers at a time when the movement itself was in its decline. It would thus be an error to see Rilke's use of negation only as a technical trick. It was an unmistakable echo of Mallarmé, and the objectivity it vouchsafed was highly significant to the evolution of Rilke's concept of the artist. Clearly, it was the symbolist position in literature which could really achieve that tenuous distinction and identification of a wholly externalized object and of the self's vision which produced it, of poetic subject matter and the poet's *persona*. Baudelaire's double visions, especially in the early sections of *Les Fleurs du Mal,* had already shown the way, but in this context Rilke was particularly touched by Mallarmé. The idea that the self objectifies the content of its consciousness precisely by withdrawing its relevance to the sensible world from which it stems provided Rilke with an important intellectual base. Such a negation goes considerably further than Keats' "Heard melodies are sweet, but those unheard are sweeter." For Rilke, as for Mallarmé, the heard melody is the artist's song turned into an "objective" vision only when it is unheard. Their unspoken association provides the thread between object and poet.

For this reason, Apollo is the most significant deity who lends distinction to an otherwise motley group of figures and themes. *New Poems* is famous for the depiction of objects: the panther, the carrousel, the Spanish dancer. But it is surprising how considerable is the bulk of prominent personae. Many are Old Testament characters; in addition to Jeremiah we find David and Saul, Jonathan, Joshua, Esther, Samuel, Absalom, and many others treated in these poems. Some poems deal also with New Testament subjects—such as the parable of the prodigal son, or the story of the resurrection—although the Old Testament poems are more clearly centered in a dominating figure. But there is also a profusion of poems on classical themes: poems on Sappho, Orpheus and Eurydice, Alcestis, Venus, Artemis, Leda, and Delphine. To be sure, these poems are outnumbered by a variety of poems on other subjects, but they are prominent among those which display a significant persona through which the Rilkean concept of self and form is developed.

In both series of *New Poems* negation often expresses itself through a specific relationship between a fixed spatial form and a scenic display or rhythmic movement. If all poems share a precarious ambivalence between motion and space, we also note a development. The very figures and organic elasticity Rilke produced in *New Poems* were canceled out by a deliberate attempt to create movement as a counter- point. It is often difficult to follow Rilke's highly intuitive reasoning, but it seems clear that he saw unfathomable relationships between the plastic form in space, in which the creative act is externalized, and its ultimate resolution in motion, eventually producing song, in which the ordering force takes part. We have already seen how this process took place in both Apollo poems. We can now see how it operates in relation to various objective figures which mirror parts or aspects of the creative act.

"Cretan Artemis" (*NP, II*), for example, shows how the luminosity of the Apollo poems can be varied and projected as a movement. Artemis in this poem is not only the huntress of antiquity but also an image of Rilke's pure, unself-conscious woman, whose virginity ex- presses her sexuality precisely because it fulfills itself through its expecta- tion. Here we confront a further involvement, because Artemis denies her very womanhood and hence also her expectancy. In the opening lines she is shown as a *thing,* an externalized object which connects her luminous brow with the objects of nature:

> Wind der Vorgebirge: war nicht ihre
> Stirne wie ein lichter Gegenstand?

As a picture, then, Artemis is *formed* by her animals, her forest, her hills. She is entirely passive. Even her gown clings to her unself-conscious breasts like a "changing premonition," in which her still absent womanhood is implied.

In the second part of the poem, however, Artemis becomes the huntress of antiquity; the picture is correspondingly dissolved into motion and she ceases to be passive, an object. As her knowing eyes look out into far distances, she is tightly girdled and cool, storming ahead with her nymphs and her hounds, bearing her bow. Absent womanhood leading to perfection has been replaced by its total denial. Only occasionally is she assailed by the cries of nature:

> manchmal nur aus fremden Siedelungen
> angerufen und erzürnt bezwungen
> von dem Schreien um Geburt.

As Artemis is again reduced to a passive state in the end of the poem, she exhibits another aspect of the poet's persona. The luminosity in the Apollo poems had suggested a negation through an absent yet somehow immanent form. But Artemis, by her very nature always in motion, suggests a different kind of denial. The artist, whom she represents, is at least occasionally overwhelmed by the forces of nature which break out despite his negation. The moment of waiting, the still expectancy of sensual bliss, which is externalized in a statuesque representation, must be ultimately surrendered.

This development is particularly evident in the great narrative poems which form a sequence toward the end of *New Poems, I*. Unlike the poems we have so far considered, which are sonnets akin to Mallarmé's, these poems at least partially return us to an earlier, more indigenously German form. "Alcestis," "Orpheus, Eurydice, Hermes," and "The Birth of Venus" hark back to preromantic German narrative verse, particularly to Schiller's poems on classical figures, despite the enormous difference in style. At the same time, they maintain a connection with the art of painting by their scenic dispositions, which remind us of nineteenth-century pictures with narrative content. But the brilliant combination of the pictorial and the dramatic, evident in all three poems, project themselves towards Rilke's later intellectual verse.

Movement, opening the way to a passage from life to death, is dramatically rendered in "Alcestis." The opening of the poem is both vivid and pictorial:

> Da plötzlich war der Bote unter ihnen,
> hineingeworfen in das Überkochen
> des Hochzeitsmahles wie ein neuer Zusatz.

The drama, of course, is provided by Admetus, the legendary husband of Alcestis, who, when asked to pay the price of his life, is relieved of death by the sacrifice of his devoted wife. Significantly, Rilke transformed Alcestis into an as yet untouched bride for whom no boundary exists between the realms of life and death. Her walk with the god's envoy into the world of death is as easy for her as the walk to the bridal bed which waits next door. For the virginal woman, whose existence is defined by her expectancy, the actuality of womanhood becomes her negation:

> Hat sie dirs nicht gesagt, da sie dirs auftrug,
> dass jenes Lager, das drinnen wartet
> zur Unterwelt gehört?

The hero through whom the poet's vision is measured is not Admetus. It is Alcestis, about to lose the purity of her expectation, who becomes both life and death. In this narrative poem the ambivalence between life and death appears not only as part of the poetic construction but also as a development of the theme.

In "The Birth of Venus" life and death are also united thematically. The visible form of the great Zeus produces motion and life. As the poem progresses, however, we realize that the life of the goddess is but an extension of the total universe she inhabits. Her beauty comprises all things as part of her illuminating shape. Indeed, her entire progress through the world of things is expressed through images of nonhuman life. Her formal beauty emerges from a loose sequence of pictures. Indeed, Venus concludes a cycle that had begun at the time she sprang from the form of Zeus. As she wanders through the world, all things—even blades of grass—turn to her in baffled amazement at her beauty. She is wholly a *picture*. This movement is underscored by Rilke's final line. Laboring in its hardest hour, the sea gives birth to a dolphin—"red, dead, and open"—the object of her transformation. Her beauty had been made possible by the elimination of life.

Venus—like Artemis and Alcestis—is not a complete representation of the poet. Like them, she reveals certain aspects of the creative act: the interchange of motion and form, life and "unlife" or death, the visible and the invisible. Beauty exists at the expense of organic life. It dwells in both realms of being and can be realized only through a negation of sensual existence which would vouchsafe its continuance in eternity. This idea is most thoroughly dramatized in Rilke's great poem, "Orpheus, Eurydice, Hermes," which anticipates the later sonnets not only in its subject matter but also in its treatment of the hero's persona.

The poem describes the familiar story of Orpheus' return from the underworld. Having charmed Persephone with his song, he is allowed to take Eurydice with him, provided he does not look back. But in Rilke's hands this familiar myth is turned in a peculiar fashion. The poet may still be somehow identified with the singer, Orpheus, but the heroine is undoubtedly the wife. As a denizen of the realm of death, she is already complete in herself, a perfect thing, far removed from the impatient husband whose song had once charmed her. While Orpheus forges impatiently ahead, his steps swallowing space, she hangs back at Hermes' arm, wholly detached. Even the light touch of the guiding god annoys her like an indiscretion. Her Great Death had filled her, and she seemed to have achieved a new maidenhood, untouchable, her sex closed like a young flower at dusk. Indeed, in her stubborn death she performs the function later attributed to Orpheus. She had dissolved into nature, becoming part of the unified life which includes both realms of being. Her long hair had surrendered like fallen rain; she had been parceled out like a hundredfold provision. She had become root. Orpheus, on the other hand, wholly disappears. When without surprise, even without a sense of tragedy at the inevitable reversal, she returns to her underworld, he is but a faint shadow hovering at the entrance. Eurydice, rather than Orpheus, performs the hero's twofold function. Having become root, she is the unitary self existing by virtue of her withdrawal from sense, by negation. But she has also entered into the world of things in which all parts of her have become aspects, or components, of the whole.

To find one's way out of the labyrinth of Rilkean thought requires Ariadne's thread. But some cardinal points emerge from a close scrutiny of some of his poems. His experience of the world as an especially inward vision counteracts his attempt to externalize his awareness as an objective representation. In *New Poems,* which are essentially spatial and pictorial, he develops the beginnings of his revised concept of the self. The hero, who is to become the Angel of the *Duino Elegies* and Orpheus of the *Sonnets,* is at first projected onto a canvas or into stone. But such a representation is insufficient. The unity achieved by a concert of things (each an independent "organism") requires a form. In poetry, this form leads to its complete expression only in song. But song can be created only when there is motion—the antithesis of painting or sculpture. The final development in most poems, therefore, has been a breaking of form, a dissolution of solid shapes to make song possible. In *New Poems* this frequently occurred through narrative action. Moreover, the juxtaposition of space and action (which will result in sound) is echoed in the world at large as a disparity between the visible and the invisible, life and death. Only an ultimate vision can reunite them, and

New Poems does not yet remove this disparity. In this collection personae usually show how spatial form can be dissolved, how heroes, and especially heroines, can be transformed into more comprehensive beings through a passive denial of life. But in the famous philosophical poems at the end of his career Rilke lent final substance to his mystical vision.

III

As we turn to the sonnets wholly dedicated to Orpheus, we are at once confronted with an insoluble problem. For as the hero's image shifts from an external representation to a state of mind, nearly insurmountable obstacles are created. As long as they are sculptures or paintings, Apollo, Artemis, Alcestis, Eurydice, and even Orpheus could exist as visually realizable forms. They are a stone statue, or an image of feminine beauty produced by plants and rocks, or a man in a blue cloak. Although their perfection is finally evoked only by negation, their existence, at least as symbols, cannot be questioned. But how can an inner perfection, an unrepresented yet felt state of mind be credibly externalized? To this difficult task the *Duino Elegies* had already been dedicated. They rendered their realms of being—Angel, man, and things—in an intellectually accessible form. In the *Sonnets to Orpheus* the idea is wholly identified with the song.

Apollo is really disconnected from his ancient prototype, because he exists only as a statue, but Orpheus becomes the actual god in his original function as bard. In the myth, Orpheus' function is twofold. The first is contained in the story of Orpheus and Eurydice, which Rilke had already treated in *New Poems*. The other, really a quite separate story, describes how Orpheus was torn to pieces by the Maenads. For Rilke, the connection between the stories is provided by music. When Orpheus was torn limb from limb, his music entered all things. We have seen enough of Rilke's tendency to discern a rhythmic unity in the profusion of independent things to realize how this idea might become a ritual enactment of poetry.

In contrasting the roles of Orpheus and Apollo, we might accept as axiomatic Erich Heller's comparison of these two figures with Nietzsche's famous pair, Apollo and Dionysus. Apollo is thus seen as the ordering force opposed to the force of mystical intoxication. The difference between Dionysus and Orpheus, Heller suggests, really reinforces the ancient affinity between them. For Rilke, the rhythmic vision produced by Orpheus' dissipation among all things is more important than the positive intoxication of the Dionysian deity.[4] But as soon as we grant the parallelism we find that Rilke moves in directions in no way charted by the author of *The Birth of Tragedy*. He is, to begin with, not really concerned with tragedy in the ordinary sense. Although, like Nietzsche, he was anxiously committed to the transcendence of dualities, he employed a characteristically opposite approach. As we have abundantly seen, any transcendence of opposites Rilke accomplished by notably passive means—through the denial not only of action but often even of presence itself. Orpheus, too, becomes significant precisely as he himself disappears, just as Apollo is important exactly as his head is removed. Moreover, Rilke's prominent display of feminine figures among ancient deities emphasizes his penchant for passivity and negation. We have observed how many of the classical heroic figures in *New Poems* are really heroines: Artemis, Alcestis, Venus, Eurydice. In Rilke's mythology the most perfect moment is that of *attente* at which a thing is about to be perfectly realized. Actuality, when it occurs, disturbs the perfection. Such a moment is closely identified with the idea of the expectant virgin. It also approaches the notion of death, for at the moment of dying the passage from life to "unlife" is similarly held in abeyance. The tragic emotion, even in its lyrical form, is therefore absent. The withdrawal of life is turned into "song."

[4] *The Disinherited Mind*, pp. 136–141 and pp. 123–177 *passim*.

Like *New Poems,* the *Sonnets to Orpheus* are a diverse lot, only
seldom relating to the figure to whom they are addressed. But, unlike
New Poems, they are thematically unified. Orpheus provides them with
a direction which is clarified in the opening sonnet of the sequence:

> Da stieg ein Baum. O reine Übersteigung!
> O Orpheus singt! O hoher Baum im Ohr!
> Und alles schwieg. Doch selbst in der Verschweigung
> ging neupeer Anfang, Wink und Wandlung vor.
>
> Tiere aus Stille drangen aus dem klaren
> gelösten Wald von Lager und Genist;
> und da ergab sich, dass sie nicht aus List
> und nicht aus Angst in sich so leise waren,
>
> sondern aus Hören. Brüllen, Schrei, Geröhr
> schien klein in ihren Herzen. Und wo eben
> kaum eine Hütte war, dies zu empfangen,
>
> ein Unterschlupf aus dunkelstem Verlangen
> mit einem Zugang, dessen Pfosten beben,—
> da schufst du ihnen Tempel im Gehör.

This is, indeed, a musical rendering of an old theme, a variation, for
example, on Baudelaire's "Correspondances." In that famous poem man
walks through nature as through a *temple* of pillars as he hears a chorus
of sounds, scents, and colors which are reflections of the infinite. Here
the temple performs a similar function and even bears a faintly similar
relation to sound. But the poet wears a particular mask: Orpheus. The
tree created by his song in the first part of the poem is converted into the
temple in the end. Both are but spatial images describing sound, for
both exist in the *ear.*

The conversions of sound into space are naturally reminiscent of
synaesthesia as advocated by Poe and the symbolists, but for Rilke they
play a more precise role. They present transformations from one kind of
being into another, essential to the artist's activity and to his concept of
himself. The use of space in the *Sonnets to Orpheus* is analogous to the

use of sound and motion in *New Poems*. Space is the counterpoint or
opposite of the bard's song. The poem opens with sounds but they are
not confused and dim, as in Baudelaire. They exist within the world, to
be confronted by a counterpoint, or negation of their own: silence.

The images in this poem simultaneously create and deny both sound
and form. Orpheus himself is present only insofar as his music had
entered all things. But this very activity leads to the intricate interchange
between the idea of sound and the images of space. The strained
expression "high tree in the ear" is the result, which shows the auditory
organ as a transplantation of music into space. A similar relationship is
created through the tree. The emerging sound shoots upward to form a
tree. Agnes Geering and Geoffrey Hartman tell us that in Rilke words
like "rising" or "towering" are often connected with transcendence.[5]
Associated with the tree, then, this kind of ascent is spatially rendered.
But it is accompanied by the word *Übersteigung* which, as Eva
Cassirer-solmitz has shown, is elsewhere attributed to music: the
transcendence through sound.[6] In their intricate juxtaposition, these
references to space and sound are brought together in spite of their
mutual antagonism.

This union of opposites is countered by a further negation. "And all
was silent." This denial is more familiar; it reminds us, in terms of
sound, of the negation we noted in the *Torso of Apollo*. The silence
creates a new beginning, which is once more turned into spatial images.
The stillness is physical; it is treated on the same level as refuge, lair, or
nest, and it is received in a hut. Finally, in the concluding tercet, the
silence produced by hearing is turned into a replica of the spatial image

[5] See Hartman, pp. 89–90. Agnes Geering connects the rising tree with the
transcendent quality of music: "Ein Gesang hebt an, der die Entfaltung des
Lebens im emporstrebenden Wachstum eines Baumes feiert: ein Gesang, der alles
je Vernommene übertrifft, eine 'reine Ubersteigung,' eine vollendete Leistung."
Versuch einer Einführung in Rilkes Sonette an Orpheus (Frankfurt a.M.: Verlag
Josef Knecht, 1948), p. 33.

[6] *Rainer Maria Rilke* (Heidelberg: G. Koester, Paul Obermüller, 1957), "Die
Sonette an Orpheus," p. 15 n.

of the beginning. The chief conversion of sound into space takes place through the ear. It is the refuge even of the dumbest animals, and their darkest desires; their dim consciousness allows the ear to be only a hut whose doorposts are trembling. But Orpheus' song orders it for them. The tree has become a *temple* in their ears.

The poems devoted to Orpheus all show similar relationships of sound and space. In the second sonnet, which presents Eurydice (as well as a young girl of Rilke's acquaintance who had recently died), Orpheus' song is again created in the ear.

> Und fast ein Mädchen wars und ging hervor
> aus diesem einigen Glück von Sang und Leier
> und glänzte klar durch ihre Frühlingsschleier
> und machte sich ein Bett in meinem Ohr.

In the third sonnet, we encounter a complete transformation of the image of Orpheus into an embodiment of pure song beyond mortal man. If in *New Poems* the purpose of transformation is usually to externalize, to render an emotion in an objectified form, here the aim is precisely the opposite. Transformation means pure song. A god may follow Orpheus through the narrow lyre, Rilke writes (once more presenting the evanescent event through a physical form), but how could a man do so? And to emphasize the distance he has come from *New Poems,* he ends the first quatrain: "At the crossing of two roads *within the heart* stands no temple for Apollo." There is no visible form which might order such an inward experience. *Song is Being,* Rilke proclaims. In this fashion, Orpheus becomes a philosophical image, a metaphor for the artist, the self, and the very mode of existence.

As Orpheus is dissolved into numbers of sound, he becomes the chiffre, or metaphor, for a unified awareness and presence of all things. As Rilke notes in his fifth sonnet: "For it is Orpheus. His metamorphosis/into this or that. We should not trouble/to find different names. Once and for all/it's Orpheus when he sings." As the large

number of sonnets in both series illustrates—most of them bearing no
direct relation to Orpheus—his infinitely pure song, which has entered
all things, recreates life, men, objects, fruits, earth, and overwhelms
machines. Song, praise, and mouth take the place of spatial form. But it
also means the surrender of Orpheus' individual identity. The metamorphosis is also a negation.

When Rilke returns to his deity in the concluding sonnets of both
series, he establishes his concepts of the self and of form without
equivocation. In I, 26, Orpheus is once more evoked as the god of order,
not Apollo's order of illumination and space susceptible to eye and
touch, but the order of motion and sound created in the ear:

> Du aber, Göttlicher, du bis zuletzt noch Ertöner,
> da ihn der Schwarm der verschmähten Mänaden befiel,
> hast ihr Geschrei übertönt mit Ordnung, du Schöner,
> aus den Zerstörenden stieg dein erbauendes Spiel.
>
> Keine war da, dass sie Haupt dir und Leier zerstör',
> wie sie auch rangen und rasten; und alle die scharfen
> Steine, die sie nach deinem Herzen warfen,
> wurden zu Sanftem an dir und begabt mit Gehör.
>
> Schliesslich zerschlugen sie dich, von der Rache gehetzt,
> während dein Klang noch in Löwen und Felsen verweilte
> und in den Bäumen und Vögeln. Dort singst du noch jetzt.
>
> O du verlorener Gott! Du unendliche Spur!
> Nur weil dich reissend zuletzt die Feindschaft verteilte,
> sind wir die Hörenden jetzt und ein Mund der Natur.

As "mouth" and "hearing" displace spatial form, so silence enacts the
role of negative space. But although the hero is transformed from an
externalized object into an inner vision, the spatial image remains as a
stubborn ingredient. It is the final aim of the *Sonnets to Orpheus* to
show the perfect balance of the order of time, on which music is based,
and the order of the body which describes the plastic form of Apollo. In

Rilke's world these two forms are the realms of the invisible and the visible of which true nature is composed.

This relationship became for Rilke a philosophical formula for a further art form, the dance. It is commonly accepted that his translation of Valéry's dialogues of Eupalinos during the early 1920's contributed materially to his conceptual progress in the *Sonnets*. The dialogue "L'Âme et la danse" is particularly relevant, because it is concerned with the identity of the spatial body and with its attempt to usurp the function of the immaterial soul. The visible and the invisible are described in a formal relation which is expressed by the musical, yet externalized, gestures of the dance. In Valéry's dialogue Socrates, Eriximachus, and Phaedrus watch the performance of an accomplished dancer at one of their banquets. Her motions elicit appropriate comments on the beauty of the body and of the soul. In his final words Socrates sums up the Rilkean idea of Orpheus:

Doubtless, the unique and perpetual object of the soul is what does not exist: what was and what is no longer; what will be and is not yet; what is possible, what is impossible—that is the soul's concern, but never, never what is.

And the body, which is what it is, see, it can no longer contain itself in space. Where shall it bestow itself? Where shall it come into being? This *one* wants to play at being *all*. It wants to play at the soul's universality. It wants to remedy its identity by the number of its actions. Being a thing, it *explodes* into events.[7]

In these words Valéry's modern Socrates restates the idea of transformation, which is the guiding principle for Orpheus. He is one, yet he is in all things. The poet-hero as the unitary body of *New Poems* has permeated the world as song. But through his death the mythical Orpheus has finally become an expression of perfect negation. Like Rilke's virginal women, he is on the brink of event. He is the purest

[7] "L'Âme et la danse," trans. Dorothy Bussy. *Valéry: Selected Writings* (New York: New Directions, 1950), pp. 197–198.

identity, including both movement and bodily form, which at this single moment are fully united. He is, then, the poet's ultimate image of himself: the ideal "lyrical 'I'." As the last sonnet of the sequence concludes:

> zu der stillen Erde sag: ich rinne
> zu dem raschen Wasser sprich: Ich bin.

IV

Rilke's conception of classical figures, especially of Apollo and Orpheus, appears, then, to have undergone a transformation. This change was heralded in *New Poems* and implied in their curious dialectic. It was amplified through the argumentation of the *Duino Elegies* and finally rendered in the *Sonnets to Orpheus*. The direction of Rilke's thought, which had begun with his technical discoveries under the guidance of Rodin, moved beyond poetic method to reach principles of his personal religion.

In Rilke's late poems the great figures of antiquity come into their own as modern representatives of man's aspirations. As he made clear in a letter of November, 1915, gods are *Satzungen* or metaphors, whose meaning and existence we accept without the need for intellectual comprehension.[8] They are an experience, a way of standing up to the overwhelming truth of nature from which ordinary mortals flinch but which poets hope to equal. The ancient gods are multiple, yet they are dominated by a single idea. Combining the one and the many, they reflect the body's desire to rival the universality of the soul. They are products of nature, yet, and this is the crux of Rilke's vision, they move gracefully between the realms of the visible and the invisible. They express nature as a whole.[9] They are also symptomatic of Rilke's oddly

[8] See Dieter Bassermann, *Der Späte Rilke* (München: Leibnitz Verlag, 1947), pp. 213–214. Rilke's definition of the divine figures as *Satzungen* includes in its initial distinction also the notion of God, particularly the medieval and mystical Christian God he had often praised in his earlier poetry.

[9] For a full discussion of this development, see "Die Götter bei Rilke," in Cassirer-Solmitz' *Rainer Maria Rilke*, pp. 1–17 *passim*.

Christian rejection of Christianity. Like many of the great mystics, he sought to combine the traditional concept of the transcendent deity with the idea of divine immanence. Orpheus, artist and god, eventually expresses this relation more fully than the God whom Rilke had celebrated in his earlier work. In *New Poems* and the *Sonnets to Orpheus,* then, innovations in poetic technique went hand in hand with Rilke's use of classical deities to depict the transformation of visible into invisible realms. The gods were the artist's material, the inmost substance of his being, as he endeavored to mold the world of things into a more comprehensive realm of existence. The ambivalence between space and sound, stasis and motion, leads to such a contemplation of man's spiritual state.

The intuitive obscurity of Rilke's thought often blurs the depth of his contribution not only to the art of poetry but also to our way of thinking about ourselves. For he has projected the figure of the poet as a heightened image of man's being, suspended as he is between an earthly and a spiritual state. At the point where these two realms meet, in the suspense of waiting for form to become event and for event to become form, man's fullest awareness of himself is realized. Only then does he contain all parts of his world, for only then is the outer world within and the inner world without. Only then is the voice of the poet an expression of human identity as a whole.

DAEDALIAN IMAGERY IN *A PORTRAIT*
OF THE ARTIST AS A YOUNG MAN

By David Hayman

J AMES JOYCE wrote his first novel in an epoch which saw the rise of modern archaeology, mythography, psychology, and in literature the spread of symbolism from France to every major country in Europe. Time was shrinking, fairytales and fictional epics were finding credence as fact, and artists were discovering in their creative spirit the reflection of past heroism. It is little wonder that Joyce, immersed as he was in a culture which traced its religion back to Rome and its race back to migrant Mediterranean princes and which hoped to see in its glorious past a reflection of a great future, should explicitly identify his fictionalized self, Stephen Dedalus, with the earliest Christian martyr and the father of artists, with Saint Stephen and Daedalus, manifestations at once of a Christian heritage and a pagan vocation but, more, of a basic tension within the hero of *A Portrait of the Artist as a Young Man*. No doubt we are doing violence to the novel and risking the fate of Mallarmé's faun when we neglect the Christian implications of the name "Stephen" for the glamorous Greek connotations of the name "Daedalus," but William York Tindall is right when he suggests that the novel's epigraph from Ovid (*Et ignotas animum dimittit in artes*) points to the prime importance of Daedalus-Icarus among Stephen's "counterparts"[1] and implies that the Daedalus parallel is as carefully worked out in the *Portrait* and as ironical as is the Odyssey-pattern which Joyce applied to *Ulysses*.

Joyce's attachment to Greek modes of thought, literature, and history has roots in his rejection of the precepts and modes of the Irish revival and the modes and dogmas of the Roman church, all of which play subsidiary roles in his books. In a sense the author has attempted to discover in the Hellenic pattern a means by which he may ennoble his own existence even while attacking what he holds dear. Drawing upon continental models at a time when his Irish contemporaries were making inbreeding a principle, Joyce found in Ibsen, Flaubert, and D'Annunzio the qualities which inform his use of the Daedalus myth. From Ibsen, a latter-day Dante, comes the stubborn heroism of the rebel and exile, the artist who persists in treating provincial themes in a reforming spirit. From Flaubert, Joyce inherited his dedication to discipline and to an aesthetic end, an end contingent upon the ironic vision which finds ugliness to be one of the components of beauty, truth to be ambivalent, and heroism relative. From D'Annunzio he derived the symbolist technique of suggesting mythological analogies for his autobiographical hero. In Joyce's favorite from among the Italian's novels, *The Flame* (*Il Fuoco*), D'Annunzio makes explicit his elaborate use of the Theseus myth to characterize the double romance and the dilemma of his egocentric hero, the poet Stelio Effrena. From this novel Joyce may also have learned of the romance of archaeology, of Schliemann's discovery of what he thought to be Agamemnon's tomb in Mycenae, a discovery which has inspired the drama that the hero of *Il Fuoco* plans to write. Significantly, or paradoxically, given the differences in the novelists' attitudes, Stelio's play (see D'Annunzio's *La Città*

---

[1] *A Reader's Guide to James Joyce* (New York, 1959), p. 74. Mr. Tindall's account of the parallels in the *Portrait* and of Joyce's use of irony in this connection is among the most provocative. See also Hugh Kenner's *Dublin's Joyce* (Bloomington, Indiana, 1956), and for a partial account of another significant parallel see Chester Anderson, "The Sacrificial Butter," *Accent*, XII (Winter, 1952).

Morta) will give expression to the native Italian genius while a Nietzschean Stephen Dedalus in his role as creator will "forge in the smithy of my soul the uncreated conscience of my race" (253).[2]

Stephen Dedalus' tale as it is developed in *A Portrait of the Artist as a Young Man* is that of a modern quest hero. Exceptionally gifted but not naturally courageous, Stephen is forced by a combination of circumstances to enter the dark regions of his soul; he is driven to free himself of delusions inherent in his condition as boy and Irishman, to form himself so that he may discover the light of his vocation. The oversensitive boy is educated in three Jesuit schools, sees his family's fortunes decline through the weakness of a father whom he at first admires and then despises. At the usual age he experiences the demands of his maturing body, and yields to them, only to repent outrageously. Sublimating his natural pride, he vows himself to fanatical piety and almost to the priesthood before he discovers his secular vocation. Finally, after testing the various aspects of his nation's sensibility and finding all of them incompatible with his needs as a budding artist, he leaves Ireland for Paris armed with secondhand clothes and what Hugh Kenner has called a neoplatonic aesthetic. The novel deals with what Joyce describes as the "curve of an emotion" deriving its aesthetic unity in part from the various analogies for the hero's development but mainly from the inner consistency of his experience of himself: his "individuating rhythm."[3] The youth who leaves Ireland at the end of

---

[2] All page references in the text refer to the Compass Books Edition of *A Portrait of the Artist as a Young Man* (New York, 1958).

[3] See Richard M. Kain and Robert E. Scholes, "First Version of the 'Portrait'," *Yale Review* (Spring, 1960), p. 360. The theory which Joyce expresses in his early essay, entitled "A Portrait of the Artist," incorporates ideas derived from his readings in Flaubert and D'Annunzio. Joyce writes, ". . . the past assuredly implies a fluid succession of presents, the development of an entity of which our actual present is a phase only. Our world . . . is, for the most part, estranged from those of its members who seek through some art . . . to liberate from the personalized lumps of matter that which is their individuating rhythm, the first or formal relation of their parts. But for such as these a portrait is not an identificative paper but rather the curve of an emotion."

the novel, reborn after a multiphase but essentially static quest, is at once maker and made, a Daedalian product of his shaping will and an Icarus shaped by the discredited Irish environment from which he imagines himself to be free. In the seond novel, *Ulysses,* a somewhat chastened Stephen has returned to Ireland with nothing more to show for his romantic exile than a handful of mannerisms and an awareness of failure: the useful knowledge that his first flight from Ireland was that of a "lapwing Icarus."

The Cretan period of the Daedalus myth provided Joyce with a classic model for the artist as hero, a portrait of the cunning, silent, and courageous innovator, the exile whose home is art and whose strength derives from the control which he exercises over his means. In the contrast or tension between the character of Daedalus and that of his son, Icarus, Joyce discovered the best analogy for the condition of becoming which characterizes Stephen as the potential artist. The figure of Daedalus, so curiously analogous to but so vastly different from the superbly erring Ulysses, is a perfect prototype for the *ideals* of a creative youth; that of Icarus is equally appropriate to youth's *achievements.*

A source of analogies for the action of the *Portrait* as well as for the hero's character and condition, Daedalus' Cretan period is rich in provocative images. The myth recounts how Daedalus, shortly after his arrival on Crete, made the cow-case that facilitated Pasiphaë's mating with the white bull of Poseidon. Later, at the command of Minos, he designed the labyrinth which housed at its center the Minotaur and his mother, while it served as a prison for the designer and as a prison and training ground for his young son. After escaping from the trap with the aid of Pasiphaë, Daedalus invented the famous wings as a means of leaving the island and with his son flew across the sea. Icarus, however, in his inexperience and pride, possessed perhaps by his untried vigor, failed to heed his father's prudent advice and flew too near the sun, melting the wax of his wings and falling to his death.

In Joyce's *Portrait* the cow, the Minotaur, and the bull, the labyrinth, the wings, the sun, and the sea all function as symbols toward which Stephen's attitudes change demonstrably as one by one in the course of five chapters he discovers and successively masters his will, his senses, his emotions, his spirit, and his intellect. The two principal images of the Daedalus myth are the two great inventions of the artificer: the labyrinth, which has at its center the male monster or Minotaur and the female force responsible for the existence of the man-beast; and the wings, which are intimately connected through Icarus with both the sun and the sea.[4]

Both labyrinth and wings are implicitly present on the *Portrait*'s second page, where the small boy, guilty of some misdemeanor, cowers under the table and is warned that "the eagles will come and pull out his eyes" (7). The table-cave, a miniature labyrinth and a self-made refuge is thus linked to the bird-monster, whose rapacity and freedom are antipathetic to the physically weak and morally unemancipated child. As elsewhere, the images, by their interaction and through Stephen's reaction to them, register the hero's condition. Before Stephen, like Daedalus, succeeds in building himself the wings which will guarantee his freedom, he builds an equally metaphorical labyrinth to protect him from the perils of freedom: a labyrinth of passageways, streets, and attitudes which shelter him from objects of his fears. Birds of a threatening nature inhabit most of the novel's first half, during which almost imperceptibly Stephen himself begins to take wing, gathering to himself the force and identity which manifests itself most clearly towards the end of the novel at the point where he begins to reject what he had hitherto taken for granted. The labyrinth, on the

[4] In the present study of Joyce's use of the Daedalus myth I intend to treat only the three most important images: the labyrinth, the minotaur, and the wings. Though the sea and the sun both figure in the novel, their role is minor and their development parallels that of the wings. Appropriately, Stephen's early experience leads to a dread of water and a fear of light which are overcome only when, in imitation of Icarus during Chapter Four, he first imagines his soul "soaring sunward" and then wades in the meandering waters left by the retreating tide.

other hand, becomes increasingly odious and threatening; the shelter becomes a trap.

Where the young Stephen, harassed by his sense of physical inadequacy, seeks shelter in the *corridors* of Clongowes Wood school, the adolescent, imbued with faith in his will as a moral force, explores *a maze of streets* to the end that he *encircles* himself in a ring of sensual vices and is *caged* by the pursuasive logic of the priestly casuists, led to repentance and toward the *hangman's noose* of the clerical vocation. Recognition of the *noose* leads him to accept life, vowing himself to the *snares* of the world. When finally he becomes aware of the dangers inherent in his condition as free soul, of the *nets* cast by society to impede his flight, he dedicates himself to self-containment—to "silence, exile and cunning"—and takes wing for Europe. Among these many terms which Joyce uses to characterize Stephen's position in relation to Daedalus' invention, the word *labyrinth* never occurs; the word *maze* occurs but once.

The corridors at Clongowes Wood are cold, damp, ill lit, haunted by specters from the past, but they provide the sensitive, weak-eyed Stephen Dedalus with shelter amidst paternal, soft-spoken priests. Though the labyrinthine quality of these passageways pervades Chapter One, it is not fully developed until the close of that chapter, when Stephen, reacting against the sadistic pandying which he has received from Father Dolan, sets out alone to complain to the rector. The boy's minor quest leads him through doors, up stairways, along the "low, dark, narrow corridor" lined with pictures of the dead to a ghost-ridden landing, into the solemn-smelling office behind the green baize door, and then back through the corridors to the playing field, the light, and the adulation of his classmates. More pronounced are the labyrinthine implications of the paths, country roads, and city streets along and through which Stephen wanders during Chapter Two, vainly attempting to sublimate his animal lusts by the exercise of his will. The climax of early adolescence is marked by the crystallization of this imagery: his entry into the poor quarters of Dublin, where, at the end of his random wandering, he encounters in a "maze of narrow and dirty streets" a whore who provides the solace which he has denied himself. Here, for the first time, he breaks with Christian discipline, entering an alien world: a shrine of Venus.

Once Stephen has recognized and experienced his manhood, the maze imagery changes in two ways. Its referents become more abstract and the metaphors more ominous: thus, for example, in the retreat chapter (III) circles suggest the labyrinthine nature of the sensual vice which gradually leads the boy to commit all of the deadly sins; cages suggest the role of the priestly casuistry which drives him to repentance; and streets with which Joyce opens and closes the chapter serve to focus these images within the established labyrinthine context. Already, at the beginning of this chapter, objective reality has given way to its internal reflection; in the following passage Stephen searches for and is repelled by images of his own lust. He is the victim not of Dublin's nighttown but of himself.

He would follow a devious course up and down the streets, circling always nearer and nearer in a tremor of fear and joy, until his feet led him suddenly round a dark corner. The whores would be just coming out . . . He would pass by them calmly waiting for . . . a call to his sinloving soul . . . Yet as he prowled . . . his senses, stultified only by his desire, would note keenly all that wounded or shamed them . . ." (102)

The adolescent's "fear and joy" reflect through ambivalence the transition of the labyrinth from shelter to trap. By the end of the last retreat sermon these emotions have turned to sheer terror and disgust so that Stephen is able to project in his imagination a convincing version of the Christian maze or hell, populating it with baroque devils. In the following description the circles have been rendered abstract. They correspond to no path or street, but at their center we may visualize the trap which is very real for the terrified boy: "Creatures were in the field . . . Goatish creatures . . . They moved in slow circles, circling closer and closer to enclose, to enclose ..." (137–138). This vision drives Stephen to complete the cycle begun when he first entered the poor quarters of Dublin: that is, to wander once again through unfamiliar and sordid streets so that he may experience in a worker's chapel, before a confession box inhabited by an incompetent Capuchin monk, the strangeness, the murmurings, and the embrace which bestows only the most temporary sort of grace: the release from the maze which is nothing more than a recommitment to it.

Between the aura of sin which pervades the opening pages of Chapter Three and the odor of sanctity on which that chapter closes occurs the novel's central episode, the retreat: a labyrinth of casuistry designed to lead young boys into the maze of moral purity. Joyce evokes the theological labyrinth as a trap for the spirit in the following descriptions of the preacher's hands as he begins the last of his sermons: "His face was kind and he joined gently the fingers of each hand, forming a frail cage by the union of their tips" (127). The labyrinthine aspect of Catholicism is confirmed in Chapter Four, where Stephen's observance of his religious duties is expressed in terms that bring to mind his former devotion to the rituals of sin: "Each part of his day, divided by what he regarded now as the duties of his station in life, circled about its own centre of spiritual energy" (147–148). The very excessive character of his piety and his humble devotion to ritual and dogma lead Stephen to an awareness of contradictions, awaken doubts whose implications soon become manifest. During his last year at Belvedere, when the hero is interviewed by the school's director, these doubts are crystallized; the priest becomes a symbol of death. We are led to associate his face with a skull and his hands with the noosed blind cord: "The priest let the blindcord fall to one side and, uniting his hands, leaned his chin gravely upon them." (157). Death ("gravely"), a priestly vocation, and the cord are as one; and Stephen, in his eagerness to escape, quickly loses himself in a new aspect of the labyrinth: ". . . the exhortation he had listened to had already fallen into an idle formal tale . . . He was destined . . .

to learn the wisdom of others himself wandering among the snares of the world" (162). Just as the hero's rejection of the fleshly devils implies his dedication to the maze of theological virtues and doubts, his rejection of the priesthood implies his commitment to the "world" in which he will have the freedom to err symbolized by the flight imagery which closes this chapter. Stephen's symbolic meeting with the "angel of mortal youth" takes place paradoxically amidst a maze of meandering waters on a Dublin beach. Foreshadowing the Greek atmosphere of Chapter Five, the emblematic bird-girl is depicted as the classical siren.

During his years at University College, Stephen finds that the "world," or at least the Irish world, makes demands which, though subtler than those made by the flesh or the church, are still dangerous to the free spirit of the would-be artist. "When the soul of a man is born in this country" he tells Davin, "there are nets flung to hold it back from flight. You talk to me of nationality, language, religion. I shall try to fly by those nets" (203). While attempting to escape these nets Stephen enters a new aspect of the maze, dedicating himself to solitary pursuits. To suggest this development Joyce has recourse once again to the maze imagery which dominated earlier chapters: to corridors, streets, and casuistry: the corridors of University College, Stephen's Academy and the streets of the Irish Athens, where the peripatetic hero indulges his taste for dialectics. But here the action is intellectual and the real world is reduced to a pale reflection of an increasingly complex mental labyrinth. Wandering freely among symbols of former bondage, Stephen is unaware of the cumulative nature of experience: of the hall of mirrors, which is his own character. When he "resolves" his problems at the close of the *Portrait* by rejecting duties and friendships, vowing himself to "silence, exile, and cunning," he brutally commits himself to a new error, an error whose nature is defined by the chaos of the journal Stephen keeps prior to his departure for France: an intellectual maze foreshadowing among other things the "Proteus" chapter of *Ulysses*.

His much vaunted self-sufficiency is useless to him as a creator unless he recognizes the stuff of his humanity.

Without its monster the labyrinth would be as incomplete as Leopold Bloom's house without Plumtree's Potted Meat. Stephen confronts beastliness under a variety of guises: as the sadistic Father Dolan, as a driving need to exercise control, as the vaguely ridiculous devils from his private hell, as the deadly vocation symbolized by the director of Belvedere and as the inconstancy and falsehood symbolized by Cranly and EC. These menaces lurk at the center of each of the various aspects of the maze, that is, near the close of each of the novel's chapters. They suggest the form of Stephen's successive delusions and mark his half-conscious recognition of them. But the monster has in each case an ironic *Doppelgänger,* a harmless-seeming twin in the sirenlike tempter whose appearance at the climax of each chapter leads Stephen to enter a new maze: the rector of Clongowes, the tender harlot, the gentle old Capuchin, the bird-girl, and Stephen's unrealistic vision of his artistic destiny.

At Clongowes Wood, Stephen confronts Father Dolan, who, by identification with his pandy-bat, which the boys call a "turkey," combines ornithic and human attributes. The uncalled-for punishment meted out by this priest weakens Stephen's faith in the inviolability bestowed by his physical weakness, his self-effacement, and his innocence. As the last in a series of disheartening events, it forces him to seek strength elsewhere, e.g., in the illusion of the power of his will. Father Dolan's infrahuman and monstrous qualities are clear even to the boy: his "whitegrey not young face, his baldy whitegrey head with fluff at the sides of it, the steel rims of his spectacles and his nocoloured eyes looking through the glasses" (50). But, though in an attempt to forestall a second encounter with the sadist he follows a miniature quest pattern and approaches the rector with trepidation and awe, Stephen fails to recognize the nature of this figure of authority seated at the cen-

ter of the maze in his solemn-smelling, silent office behind a desk surmounted by a skull. He mistakes administrative hypocrisy for nobility
and justice. The rector like the whore, the Capuchin confessor, and the
bird-girl-siren, seems benign; like those other implicit monsters he
greets the hero, saves him from a more easily recognized menace, and,
however unintentionally, sends him forth laden with false hope into a
new maze.

The most Daedalian of all the allegorical beasts and perhaps the most
significant is the monster of lust which the hero confronts in nighttown
but fails to recognize before the retreat sermons of Chapter Three.[5]
Stephen's sexual needs are gratified after his frustrated desire sends him
moaning "to himself like some baffled prowling beast" (99) through the
"maze" of streets to the harlot in whose "arms he felt that he had
suddenly become strong and fearless and sure of himself" (101).
Products of his monstrous delusion, this new-found strength and
certainty are impermanent, derived from the air, from the perfumes of
the whores and the semiritualistic setting. The harlot is a deceptively
beautiful projection of Stephen's own beastliness and weakness. Perhaps
she is also the female partner of the bull; as such she is prefigured by the
cows of Chapters One and Two and in her turn she prefigures the dirty
old woman of Chapter Three, who in a similar street shows Stephen the
way to his next monstrous tempter. Her love-magic, though performed
before the timeless altar, is inefficacious when matched with the
Christian concept of sin and hell and with Stephen's own pride.

[5] We should note here that Joyce's conception of the minotaur of lust is
probably derived from Dante's view of that beast as expressed in Canto XII of
the *Inferno*. There the monster personifies "violence, bestiality, and lust" and
guards the entrance to the seventh circle. The imagery of circles used by Joyce
owes much to Dante's vision of hell though this fact need not alter the
labyrinthine implications of the references cited above. The *Divine Comedy*, like
Goethe's *Faust* and Renan's *Life of Jesus*, simply constitutes a further parallel for
aspects of Stephen's development.

Consequently, after first experiencing sin and then, as a result of the retreat sermons, exaggerating his guilt, Stephen has hallucinations. He sees in the debased Christian version of the Minotaur [6] the beastliness which lurked behind his first sinful action:

Creatures were in the field; one, three, six: creatures were moving in the field, hither and thither. Goatish creatures with human faces, horny browed, lightly bearded and grey as indiarubber. A malice of evil glittered in their hard eyes, as they moved hither and thither, trailing their long tails behind them. (137)

The moment of truth experienced at the carnal center of Dublin has been complemented by the discovery of Stephen's own carnal center. Recognizing the beast with whom he has been doing battle, the boy turns toward the extreme of humility and repentance, toward the old bearded monk who sits caged in his confessional, a living symbol of the vocation which he is later to recognize as a form of death.

As Stephen matures, the minotaur image tends like the other images in the novel to reverse itself. Thus, in Chapter Four, the director of Belvedere with his skull and noose resembles the implicitly monstrous rector of Clongowes, but the director is recognized by Stephen as a menace and equated by the reader with other explicit monsters. Paradoxically, the boy turns for solace to allegorical beasts, ironic parallels for the pandy-bat–wielding Father Dolan. Stephen greets with

[6] That Joyce means these panlike devils to be minotaur figures is clear enough from the context, the general development of the mythological theme, and the boy's reactions. However, here as elsewhere, the author has deliberately introduced foreign elements. It may even be that Joyce has cribbed many of the aspects of the central monster and much of what Stephen experiences in Chapter Three from the storehouse of similar materials available in D'Annunzio's novels and especially in *Il Fuoco,* where, for example, Stelio Effrena experiences while wandering in the artificial maze a "torpid burning inside him, from his most remote origin, from a primitive bestiality, from the ancient mystery of sacred libidinous desires . . ." We note that D'Annunzio, like Joyce, links the faun to the labyrinth and the labyrinth to outrageous sensuality and sadism.

elation his vision of the bird-man Daedalus and the bird-girl; [7] for, once he has faced, recognized, and overcome the monster of lust, traditional beasts of allegory and myth lose their horror for him, becoming, during his Grecian phase, symbols of the freedom of the spirit, a freedom whose limits he has yet to apprehend. These fused entities embody after all some of the contradictions inherent in reality; they symbolize for Stephen the "gates of all the ways of error and glory" (172). He fears in their stead a new sort of monster, the benign-seeming agents of a society which has designs upon his liberty: the director of Belvedere, the wingless bird-man or false priest Cranly or the batsouled EC. As a result he tumbles with predictable consistency into new errors, mistaking as before the siren for the angel, the labyrinthine or protean confusion of his journal for the birth pangs of the free spirit, Circe's pigsty of the subconscious for a field of daisies.

The role of wing and bird images in the *Portrait* is strikingly different from that of either the labyrinth or the Minotaur. For, from slight but ominous beginnings, the references to feathered creatures and flight fan out to dominate the imagery of the last two chapters of the novel. It is almost as though through the distribution of this image Joyce wished to suggest the form of a wing which by the close of the book is massive enough to carry Stephen to Europe if not to artistic achievements of moment.

The narrow tip of this Daedalian wing is feathered with awesome bird images. First the eagle threatens to "pull out" Stephen's eyes; then the "greasy leather orb [which] flew like a heavy bird" (8) across the playing field at Clongowes drives him into the shelter of the school's corridors. Even the turkey served at Stephen's first Christmas dinner takes on unpleasant connotations by association both with the dinner

[7] It is ironical that the most Greek of the monsters (the siren-harpy-bird-girl) belongs to the context of another myth and foreshadows Stephen's relationship to Bloom-Ulysses. But the girl, by her cranelike aspect, calls to mind the labyrinthine crane dance performed by Theseus on Crete.

and with Mr. Barrett's pandy-bat or "turkey," an instrument which later justifies this analogy. For the physical distress occasioned by the beating Stephen receives from Father Dolan matches in its intensity the emotional impact of the fateful dinner. In spite of these unpleasant connotations, Stephen is obliquely identified with birds at the close of Chapter One, after he has successfully confronted the rector in his office. Walking across the playing field, the boy is greeted by his fellows who, "flinging their caps again into the air and whistling as they went spinning," made "a cradle of their locked hands and hoisted him up among them and carried him along until he struggled to get free" (59). The flight of the caps, the boy's cries, the lifting up, and the mention of freedom, all are echoed in later flight sequences. But, as Stephen is not prepared for flight, it is the caps which fly accompanied by the "whistling" birdcalls of the boys; the childish hero, lifted in a "cradle," fights flight. Returning to the ground, he thinks about turnips and humility rather than of his glorious destiny. His fear of birds amounts to a fear of freedom or, rather, an innate but repressed craving for freedom. The incident represents metaphorically his first fleeting triumph over the evil birds, the first stage in Icarus-Daedalus' preparation.

During the next period of Stephen's childhood the evil associations of birds are carried by the first of his alter egos, the rival and tempter, Vincent Heron, who has "a bird's face as well as a bird's name" (76). A figure of pride and rebellion, Heron subjects Stephen to violent treatment on two occasions and tries to seduce him from "his habits of quiet obedience," threatens, that is, to upset the boy's precarious moral balance. It is to this dark bird that Stephen unwittingly capitulates at the end of Chapter Two when he enters nighttown in search of solace to discover moral degradation. A second metaphorical flight occurs in the "maze" of streets shortly before the hero "resolves" his dilemma in the harlot's embrace: "He stretched out his arms in the street to hold fast the frail swooning form that eluded him and incited him: and the cry that he had strangled for so long in his throat issued from his lips. It broke from him like a well of despair from a hell of sufferers and died in a wail of furious entreaty . . ." (100). In such a context the outstretched arms, the ambivalence of the boy's aspirations, and the lewd cry which frees itself evoke the flight of a Luciferian being, the naysayer.

Among the extravagant metaphors of the retreat chapter (III) we find images which contribute to or foreshadow the subsequent reversal of Stephen's position in regard to birds, his acceptance of the wings. We note, for example, the peacock of pride and the pigeon of humility, the wings of good angels and those of Lucifer. At the chapter's close Stephen's prayers (winged spiritual emissaries) are seen to stream toward heaven "from his purified heart like perfume" (145) immediately before the boy, unconscious of his emblematic fall, strides homeward along "gay" but "muddy streets."

The fourth chapter of the *Portrait* could be called "the Epiphany of the Dove." In its opening section Stephen contemplates "with trepidation . . . the unseen Paraclete, Whose symbols were the dove and a mighty wind, to sin against Whom was a sin beyond forgiveness . . ." (148-149). By the close of the chapter the youth has rejected the priestly vocation, experienced the "wind" through the illusion of flight and contemplated with *joy* the "darkplumed dove," his "angel of mortal youth and beauty." The most Daedalian of Stephen's flights and falls occurs toward the end of the chapter while he walks across the beach. Inspired by the sound of his own name, he is lifted upon imaginary wings:

His heart trembled; his breath came faster and a wild spirit passed over his limbs as though he were soaring sunward. His heart trembled in an ecstasy of fear and his soul was in flight . . . An ecstasy of flight made radiant his eyes and wild his breath and tremulous and wild and radiant his windswept limbs . . . His throat ached with a desire to cry aloud, the cry of a hawk or eagle on high, to cry piercingly of his deliverance to the winds. This was the call of life to his soul . . . (169)

Stephen interprets this *flight* as a call to "create proudly out of the freedom and power of his soul, as the great artificer whose name he bore" (169–170). This metaphorical ascent of the spirit or "soul" takes Stephen too near the sun and blinds him to the realities of existence and of the artist's craft. As usual he fails to note the Icarian fall, which occurs when with a "lust of wandering in his feet" he wades along the course of the "long rivulet in the strand" toward the bird-girl. Purified of the taint of the church and of the flesh, the wading bird-girl represents the secular mystery of life. As the winged creation of the winged creator she is the embodiment of the beauty which Stephen feels within his newborn soul. But more precisely she is a siren, a combination of dove, crane, and woman, whom Stephen mistakingly identifies with earth's bounty and the freely bestowed gift of expression. Though the youth's reactions to the bird imagery of this sequence are positive, the images themselves are ambivalent. Stephen identifies with Daedalus as the solar hawk (see Egyptian god Ra) but also with the eagle which threatened him in Chapter One and drove him into his first metaphorical labyrinth. The girl who enchants him and seduces his spirit is at once a black dove and a lunar bird; the crane is after all a cousin of the ibis, symbol of the moon-god Thoth.

In Chapter Five, the young student at University College acquires the learning, the skill, the understanding, and the confidence which will eventually free him of the provincial bias and establish for him the validity of his new purpose, serve as wings, that is, with which he can fly all that would limit his powers. Though he fails to reconcile the contradictions inherent in the wing imagery and the Daedalian identity or to fulfill their promise, he accepts the wings as a part of his life, identifies them with freedom and with the need for an exile, which he finally achieves with the aid of a ship whose sails are a practical substitute for the wings of fancy. Aside from the early reference in this chapter to flying by the Irish nets, and another to the Irish nation's batlike soul, the most obvious bird and wing images are found in the penultimate section of Chapter Five, during which Joyce destroys in Stephen the illusions created on the beach in Chapter Four. Here, armed with the augurs' rod and searching the sky for portents in the manner of a Greek seer, Stephen expresses along with his distrust of winged symbols his growing awareness of personal failure: "A sense of fear of the unknown moved in the heart of his weariness, a fear of symbols and portents, of the hawklike man whose name he bore soaring out of captivity on osierwoven wings, of Thoth, the god of writers" (225). The vision of the bird-girl predicted to Stephen the achievement of his creative destiny in Ireland. In Chapter Five Stephen's birdlike friends affirm the impossibility and impracticality of that dream— identifying Ireland with the trap. Cranly, the faithless but demanding friend, is joined in Stephen's mind with EC, the bat-souled and inconstant lover. Together this bat and crane constitute proof of the uncreated nature of the Irish conscience and confirm him in his vocation, help motivate his exile by forcing him to recognize himself as a stranger on Irish Crete. Stephen's growing familiarity with wings and winged beings, his metaphorical preparations for flight are climaxed by the lyrical journal entries dated April 16 and 27. In the first of these, after hesitation and a great deal of talk, the hero flaps Byronic and Baudelairean pinions along with his "brothers," the "tall ships that stand against the moon" shaking "the wings of their exultant and terrible youth" (253). Eleven days later these exultant drumbeats and buglecalls, designed no doubt to lift waning morale, are feebly echoed as the youth prepares to put to sea. His last cry is a plea to Daedalus: "Old father, old artificer, stand me now and ever in good stead" (253). The hero's flight, that of a "lapwing Icarus," is inauspicious; but as his confusion in Ulysses would indicate, the fall will not be from sun to sea but from youth and romantic fancy, from the romantic or *fin de siècle* illusion of absolute purity into the sea of life and the chaos of ideas and existences.[8] The boy who in desperation calls upon a mythological father is hardly ready to accept freedom, to use his wings, to become the maker—hardly aware of the nature of his own commitments.

As we have seen, the images outlined above are a constant in the Portrait in that each chapter has its labyrinth, monsters, and birds or wings. Thus in Chapter One corridors are labyrinthine, Father Dolan is monstrous, and Stephen is lifted in simulated flight by his classmates. In Chapter Two the labyrinthine streets lead Stephen to a recognition of beastly yearnings, to a mock flight and a fall into the arms of a harlot. The ecclesiastical hell with its monstrous inhabitants is the labyrinth of Chapter Three, which ends with the adolescent's elevation through prayer. The maze of theological inconsistencies leads Stephen to recognize the danger of the priestly vocation offered to him in Chapter Four. This chapter concludes with Stephen's identification with the spirit of flight, through art, as personified by Daedalus-Icarus. As student at University College, in an intellectual setting reminiscent of fifth-century Athens, the youth explores an intellectual and social labyrinth, discovers the monster of Irish infidelity, from which he flies on a winged ship. In terms of the Daedalian pattern each chapter epitomizes Stephen's total progression, creating an aura of inevitability which contributes to the aesthetic stasis of the novel. Meaningful repetitions and cross references enable Joyce to re-enforce the idea that his hero is repeatedly remaking himself through a series of deaths and rebirths which can hardly end with Stephen's departure from Ireland.

Viewed in the perspective of the novel as a whole, the Daedalus patterns of the chapters contribute to a more emphatic progression. In the *Portrait* as in the myth, the building of the labyrinth precedes the

[8] This cluster of winged images, Stephen's dedication to the aesthetic ideals of the decadents, and the preciosity of his early creative output lead to the impasse exposed during *Ulysses*. The climax of the later novel occurs when Stephen, breaking a "mauve" lampshade, breaks with nineteenth-century aestheticism and Icarus prior to joining his destiny with that of the prudent Bloom.

encounter with the monster; the flight follows the escape from the trap. Accordingly the most emphatic reference to the labyrinth, the "maze of ... streets," occurs in Chapter Two; the most concrete man-beast image, the faunish devils, appear in Chapter Three; and the clearest reference to flying, and indeed to the Daedalian parallel, occurs in Chapter Four. This sequence of symbolic occurrences may be variously interpreted, but the most likely account of the Daedalus myth as a parallel for the plot of the *Portrait* would make of Simon Dedalus the fabulous father who, by his financial and personal ruin, brings his unfortunate son during the book's second chapter into the maze or trap of poverty, and places him under obligation for the dangerous charity of the church. In this case the maze chapters are two, three, and four, during which Stephen struggles, first, against his injured pride of position; then, against his sense of propriety; thirdly, against the ascendency of his senses; and finally, against his spiritual doubts and his obligation to uphold the tenets of the church. In the course of these three chapters Simon is replaced by the priests, who as surrogates for the Divine Creator apparently save Stephen in Chapter Three from the terrors which infest the center of the labyrinth. These father-surrogates guide him away from the monster of lust which he has discovered in himself and from the damnation which could be his fate. The awful center is graphically described during the retreat sermons and more graphically experienced during the infernal or monstrous vision, which forces Stephen to retrace his steps so that he may exorcise completely his demon. By releasing the hero temporarily from his sense of guilt and permitting him to devote himself whole-heartedly to the intricacies of piety and dogma, the confession leads Stephen imperceptibly out of the labyinth toward the acceptance of life and of his artistic vocation. The latter takes place during the bird-girl passage, which most critics consider the novel's climax. In the meantime the Divine Father and his surrogates have been replaced by the inspiring image of the "hawklike man" Daedalus, symbolizing for Stephen a yet undefined type of artistic creator, a secular god with whom he sees fit to identify. This escape from the cares of the impoverished and life-denying intricacies of the church is signalled by the illusion of flight which functions as part of the glory of the light greeting the hero when he finally emerges from the trap to resume life in the open upon the enemy isle of Crete. It also serves to foreshadow Stephen's flight from an island which persists in wishing to confine his spirit. Stephen's flight from Ireland must result in an Icarian fall. *Ulysses,* the record of his floundering in the sea of life, recounts his anguished search for form and direction in this chaotic medium.

This progression, superficially so satisfying and nearly identical with that of the myth, answers many of the questions raised by Stephen's name and by the Daedalian imagery. However, it fails to account for the fact that Stephen shares his identity not only with Icarus and Daedalus but also with a number of other figures, that in moments of exaltation he himself is half-aware of these identities though he is incapable of interpreting them accurately and dispassionately, and that these parallels along with the appropriate activities are not terminated before the end of *Ulysses.*

The virtues peculiar to Stephen's several analogues are too disparate to permit us to equate his various roles. They contribute however to a more vital aspect of the hero, his identity as all-hero, a quality which is paralleled in *Ulysses* by the portrait of Bloom as everyman or the prototype of humanity. Thus, we may equate salient qualities of Daedalus and Icarus with the extremes in art and see in their conjunction, that is in Stephen, the ideal through unstable mean or the type of the artist-hero. As a combination of Daedalus and Icarus, Stephen personifies the two aspects of the artist's vision: his gift of immediate lyrical expression as evidenced by Icarus' flight to the sun and the fall into the sea; the control which the Daedalian artist must exercise over that gift if he is to render its fruit valid as art. Daedalus' control is suggested by the nature of his flight which takes him safely between sun and sea. Here, by Joyce's own definition, we have the impulsive romantic temperament harnessed to the controlled classical temper, an unstable and ironic marriage which accounts for incongruities in Stephen's character as an aspiring artist but most particularly for his inability in the novel's last chapter to apply his growing critical insight to his creative output. (See the "romantic" poem which he writes immediately after expounding his "classic" theories to Lynch [216–224].) A similar Faustian fusion of ideal and force, but on a totally different plane, is implied by the Christ-Lucifer identity, wherein two types of revolt are manifest in Lucifer's egocentricity and Christ's sacrifice and are permitted to unite at intervals in the human expedient. In spite of complex and often profound similarities Lucifer is not Icarus; neither is Christ a maker. One set of identities vibrates in one direction, toward the human faculty to create and to create even divinely or ideally; the other set operates in the sphere of social and spiritual action and reaction. The two sets may be seen as alternate rays of Stephen as potential. That is, if we take Stephen as the center of a star, the identities are his vitality and his brilliance.

Finally, through the use of the Daedalus myth Joyce seems to illustrate Stephen's fundamental weakness, a weakness which is perhaps corrected in *Ulysses* through the joining of his identity to that of Bloom. Until Daedalus and Icarus (and Lucifer and Christ) are reconciled or synthesized in Stephen's mind, until he recognizes in himself the element of humanity and acknowledges the values with which he is surrounded and his own intellectual and emotional commitment to those values, until, that is, he recognizes the nature of the labyrinth as an essential aspect of man's condition, he will not be able to use the wings or realize his potential as artist and as human being. Even the bitter discovery of his Icarian identity reflected in the following statement from *Ulysses* will not help much unless he accepts both halves of his creative being as equally valid: "Fabulous artificer the hawklike man.

You flew. Whereto? Newhaven-Dieppe, steerage passenger. Paris and back. Lapwing. Icarus. *Pater, ait.* Seabedabbled, fallen, weltering." [9] Stephen, who throughout his life has searched for the stability embodied in the person of a father, who has implicitly recognized that need in his Icarian cry, "Old father, old artificer, stand me now and ever in good stead," can solve his dilemma only by achieving the father which is within him, by reconciling himself with his past, accepting his present, and thus freeing himself for the future. We need not ask whether Stephen ever accomplished this so long as the conditions of freedom have been stated.

[9] *Ulysses,* Modern Library (New York, 1934), p. 208.

KAZANTZAKIS' *ODYSSEY*

By Frederic Will

MODERN Greek literary culture is no longer seen wholly in the shadow of antiquity. The creative power of postclassical Greek literature has been making itself felt in recent years. Translations into English have become common, and now constitute, along with the brief commentaries on that material, a substantial introduction in English to the literature of modern Hellenism. Names like Solomos, Palamas, Sikelianos, Cavafis, and Seferis are now well known, and respect for their achievements is widespread, at least among the literarily interested in this country.

Not until recently, however, has the full scope and demand of that literary achievement been suspected here. Previously we had known lyric or longer narrative poems, and a few novels. Nothing epic—in any sense of the word—had been brought to our attention. In 1958 appeared a translation of Nikos Kazantzakis' *Odyssey,*[1] which has en-

[1] I am largely dependent, here, on the translation of Kazantzakis' *Odyssey* by Kimon Friar (New York, 1958), as well as upon stimulation from Mr. Friar. This fine translation—admittedly I have checked it with the original only at a few points—brings us closer to one of our major twentieth-century writers. We have translations of several other Kazantzakis works into English: *Zorba the Greek, Freedom or Death,* and *The Greek Passion.*

larged and deepened our notion of the modern Greek achievement. That modern epic, in 33,333 lines, is based on Homer's *Odyssey*. It literally takes its beginning from the end of Homer's poem. Kazantzakis' Odysseus, furthermore, has much in common with Homer's hero. That is not all. Even the "godlike" vision of Homer is emulated. Here it is not a question of evaluating Kazantzakis: I, for one, am prepared so far only to speak of the work as huge in scope and impressive, not as a classic. It is simply that Kazantzakis strives for the history-and-essence-embracing wholeness of vision which we associate with Homer. Homer is challenged. One feature of that challenge concerns me here.

From the beginning Kazantzakis' Odysseus differs in an obvious way from Homer's hero: he tends more toward change, toward becoming different in nature through the course of his wanderings. As we read on, we find this a limited difference; similarities crop up on all sides. But the difference tells us much in the present case.

From our first meeting with Homer's Odysseus, on Calypso's island, to our final encounter on Ithaca, after he has defeated the suitors, we find him essentially "unchanging." This becomes clear when we think back over the chief scenes involving Odysseus: with Calypso, with the Phaeacians, with Circe, with the Cattle of the Sun, with the swineherd, or with the suitors. Each time, although the circumstances differ, the "character" of Odysseus remains basic, keeps the same psychic figure. "He" is identical with himself. Naturally this identity is hard to analyze, and even harder to describe, because Homer has dramatized Odysseus' character into him, from within. That "character" is thoroughly organic, lacks obtrusive traits to be observed, noted, and set aside analytically. Still we can try to corral that character with nouns: something which we may call Odysseus' vitality, canniness, courage, and pride remain consistently at the felt core of his behavior. They are changeless.

The hero of Kazantzakis' epic is somewhat different. "Something" in him is constant. Certainly the author's vision has been steady and persistent. But his Odysseus changes—essentially and variously—in a way Homer's hero does not.

That change takes the form of a gradual release from "society," in a broad sense, from the pressures of social conventions, from the constraints of family affection, from all routine social occupations. The progress of this release is not unilinear, does not head straight for the mark; but throughout it can be felt as a thrust. When Odysseus first returns to Ithaca, has destroyed the suitors, and presents himself to Penelope, he is still relatively involved in the social web. He is far from docile, having just returned from the wars, and has fought like a bull to save his property and house. But he can still wonder at not feeling the old love for Penelope: he is sufficiently part of his past to remember:

> "O heart, she who for years has waited you to force
> her bolted knees and join you in rejoicing cries,
> she is that one you've longed for, battling the far seas,
> the cruel gods and deep voices of your deathless mind."
> He spoke, but still his heart leapt not in his wild chest.
>
> (I, 30–34)

His relation to Telemachus is similarly strained, tense between former fondness and present coolness. Although he has passed beyond a sentimentally paternal attitude, and sees more nearly *sub specie aeternitatis,* he still feels for his son. When Odysseus speaks (I, 167 ff.) of the need for brutality, in order to subdue mutinous subjects, Telemachus objects: he is milder than his father, and would like to rule his people gently. Though the father at first resents this opposition, he checks himself, realizing that he respects opposition. Recalling an occasion when he had fiercely crossed his own father, he thinks of the way the generations must replace each other:

> Gently he touched with love his son's mane, raven-black:
> "Ah, lad, I feel your pain, and I love your sharp impatience,
> but hold your wrath: all things shall come, all in their turn.

I've done my duty as a son, surpassed my father,
now in your turn surpass me both in brain and spear . . ."

(I, 203–207)

Here as with Penelope Odysseus expresses a love, as though from a great distance, from the other side of pain and experience. But he feels his deepest relation to his father. That man's death determines him (I, 599 ff.) finally to arrange for Telemachus' marriage and his own departure. It is clear that Odysseus has always felt closer to his father than to his son. One of his tenderest actions is the burial of Laertes:

> . . . then last of all he masked his father's holy face
> with pure gold leaf, marked out his lashless eyes, his mouth,
> his thorny eyebrows, long mustaches, cheeks and chin,
> and bending over the tomb cried thrice his father's name,
> but it went lost, and no loved echo rose from earth.

(II, 590–594)

Kazantzakis has carefully integrated heroic restlessness into these suggestions of Odysseus' lingering domestic feeling. There is little more than mention, in Homer, of Teiresias' prophecy that Odysseus must continue to wander, after he reaches home, and that he will settle down only in old age. That mention, which inspired Dante and Tennyson to the vision of Odysseus as an "eternal wanderer," [2] becomes a seminal motif for Kazantzakis: he does not mention the prophecy, but he uses its spirit. Odysseus' antipathy to the bourgeois situation on Ithaca is brought out subtly. It is chiefly shown, as in the relationship with Telemachus and Penelope, by a dramatized sense that Odysseus has gone beyond, has transcended the kinds of existence he finds on Ithaca, where there has been no war, no heroism, no maturing. At home Odysseus finds dying old men, feckless suitors, lascivious maids, a frightened, binding wife, and a prudish, if determined, son. In contrast

---

[2] For a useful survey of interpretations of Odysseus in literature, cf. W. B. Stanford, *The Ulysses Theme* (Oxford, 1954).

to Homer, Kazantzakis brings out the impossibility of any real domestic reunion, precisely through the scene in which Odysseus retells his wanderings to Penelope and Telemachus. During this narrative, in Book II, there is little rapport between Odysseus and his hearers, much less, for instance, than between Homer's Odysseus and Penelope, for in those Homeric scenes a mutually ironic understanding between speaker and listener is felt. Odysseus seems to be talking to himself, taking stock of his situation. But it is not until the end of his narrative that we realize how completely he has convinced himself, in telling of his former freedom, of the importance of remaining free. We read, at the end of the narrative:

> Odysseus sealed his bitter lips and spoke no more,
> but watched the glowering fire fade, the withering flames,
> the ash that spread like powder on the dying coals,
> then turned, glanced at his wife, gazed on his son and father,
> and suddenly shook with fear, and sighed, for now he knew
> that even his native land was a sweet mask of Death.
>
> (II, 42 ff.)

Surrounded by a group of fellow adventurers, Odysseus leaves Ithaca for the horizon. At this point his relation to his men—Captain Clam, Kentaur, Hardihood, Orpheus, and Granite—is of little importance. They will only later take their part in a more evolved stage of the relationships into which Odysseus enters. He turns first to Helen, in the gradual weaning of himself from the familial. She will tie a less dangerously holding bond to him than his family once did.

Traveling south to Sparta, Odysseus and his men come to Menelaus' palace. There they find the old king gone soft, living self-indulgently on his lands while his serfs starve. Odysseus is disgusted. Helen has kept her flame alive, however, and love instantly flares up. It is important to see, though, that Kazantzakis does *not* stress the sexual relation between Helen and Odysseus. This neglect brought inevitable criticism against

the author.[3] But it was intentional and appropriate neglect. Odysseus
has passed the stage of sentimental eroticism. Furthermore, the intimacy
of a sexual bond would have drawn his nature too strongly back toward
"society." Just as he rejoiced in Telemachus' self-realization in manhood,
so he rejoices here in Helen's rediscovered power to represent the
eternally love-worthy woman. Her warmth radiates to him. But he is
careful not to burn himself.

The looseness of their relationship grows clearer in the following
books (IV–VIII). Helen, Odysseus, and Odysseus' men go to Crete,
where they stay at length with an old Trojan War friend, Idomeneus.
He is an old man, in constant need of bull-rites and ritual intercourse in
order to vitalize his sagging body. Around him, spawn of an egregiously
decadent society, cluster the aristocratic leaders of Crete. During their
long stay in this environment Odysseus and Helen grow progressively
farther from one another; they separate. Although Helen, as much as
Odysseus, has been revolted by Idomeneus, and by his lascivious designs
on her, she has not fallen back on Odysseus for help. From the time of
her arrival on Crete she has been attracted to a blond farmer by
whom—Odysseus not protesting—she becomes pregnant. Odysseus
himself seeks for health—escape from the dissolution of Cnossos—in
another direction. His motive, here again, is the kind of abstract
defence of vitality which earlier led him to rejoice in Telemachus'
self-discovery. Now he puts his faith in the blond Dorian invaders, who
had already impressed him at Sparta, and plots with them and his own
comrades to destroy the civilization of Cnossos. The plot is successfully
and brutally carried out: the palace of Cnossos is burned to the ground,
and few survivors are left among the decadent. Odysseus has followed
out his own vital convictions consistently. The Dorian "barbarians," in

[3] Kazantzakis replied: "You do not see the obvious: Helen's abduction by
Odysseus was not an erotic one. Helen was stifling in Sparta, and she longed to
leave; Odysseus wanted to take her with him as a new Trojan horse, to lean
her against the disintegrating civilization of Knossos in order to destroy it" (cited
by Friar, p. 819).

their pristine wholeness, are left to take over. Meanwhile Odysseus has moved spiritually far from Helen.

It is hard for Odysseus to leave Helen, who of course is spared, with her farmer, in the holocaust. Odysseus has not entirely freed himself from sentimental affection. As he watches her for the last time, standing beside her husband, he says:

> "Helen, belovèd face of earth, these eyes of mine
> Shall never see you more, nor these rude hands caress you;
> on my mind's peak you rose like glittering foam, and vanished."
> He spoke, then turned his face, not to reveal his tears . . .
>
> (VIII, 916 ff.)

But he has always been less involved with Helen than with his family. His relation to her has had more of bravura and mere experiment. It is not five minutes before he has cast off, this time for Egypt.

The next four books (IX–XII) are an interlude, from the viewpoint of the main argument. Those books involve the adventures of Odysseus and his men in Egypt, adventures which eventually lead them down the Nile to Thebes, where a besieged Pharaoh becomes the center of their fortunes. Now our attention is on Odysseus: as he fights—though with misgivings—on the side of the revolutionaries, is wounded and jailed, eventually escapes, and, gathering most of his original comrades together, sails farther down the Nile toward Black Africa. The details of the narrative are irrelevant here.

Two points concern the argument. It is of interest, first, that Odysseus grows increasingly aware of "metaphysical" conditions which bear on his relation to society, to other people. Those conditions are aspects of the true severity of the world, especially of the world of inanimate nature. His growing awareness of these conditions is signaled by an announcement, shortly after he and his men arrive in Egypt, that

> "the more I roam this earth and spread my claws, the more
> I feel that the herald of my hunting god is Hunger.

Forward! It's time to cut the river's current, brothers,
for I divine before us much of God, much more of Hunger!"
(IX, 236–239)

In the following book, calling on art to express his growing sense of the
austerity of existence, Odysseus fashions an image of his God, "a
lumpish dwarf/ gray hair and beard, blood-clotted eyes, huge ears and
teeth . . ." (X, 780–781). It is only in Book XI, however, that this theme
is fully developed. There, imprisoned by the Pharaoh, Odysseus tries for
days to carve an adequate statue of his god. He is frustrated at first by
his tendency to represent himself, in various guises; naively to represent
the human, and to worship it as transcendent. Finally, however,
Odysseus began to create:

> . . . [the] chips flew,
> the eyes became deep wells, the great skull a hard flint,
> the brows a rock-strewn cliff, the mouth a deep dark cave,
> and the wrenched lips hung loose and yowled like a wild beast's.
> (XI, 866 ff.)

This god, whom Odysseus shortly after calls the "great God of Vengeful
Wrath!" (l. 892), is his final product.

In view of these metaphysical-aesthetic experiments it hardly sur-
prises us to find Odysseus, in the corresponding books (IX–XII), still
further cutting his sentimental ties to other people. Apart from relationships to various revolutionary Egyptians, with whom he contracts no
friendship, but only a kind of abstract sympathy, the original comrades
are his entire social context. They do still smack to Odysseus of Ithaca,
of mutual experiences, of crises surmounted, and of a once congenial
Weltanschauung. But this is little more than an aura surrounding the
men, and Kazantzakis carefully confines it to that. The men themselves—with their symbolic names, and their abstractly representative
personalities—provide little warmth for Odysseus, much less than
Helen did. They are echoes from a society of which Odysseus was once
a part. They too are casting off from society, but their sense of mission is

much less articulate than his; he cannot commune with them. As a result, Odysseus comes simultaneously to realize the true inhumanity of existence, and the impossibility, in a wider sphere than he had before known it to apply, of his contracting close human relationships.

From here on, all familiar social contacts begin to weaken and grow meaningless to Odysseus. He is still followed by his companions, as he travels farther into Africa. Despite their occasional defections—to become a native king (Kentaur), or tribal chieftain (Rocky)—most of the original group are with their leader when he reaches the lake-source of the Nile (end of Book XIII). But Odysseus' vital relation is no longer with these men; it is with the band of riff-raff who have followed him out of Egypt. His relation to them is creative and mastering, in one sense; it is also the most abstract, principle-based relation that we have seen Odysseus adopt toward others.

The group of impoverished, mutilated, or socially unacceptable Egyptians have followed Odysseus out of mere despair and mere hope. They too have been victims of Pharaoh's tyranny. They are also following Odysseus' vision of a place

> where wheat grows tall as trees, and weeds to a man's height,
> and the pig-thistle springs beyond a horse's rump.
>
> (XI, 1323–1324)

There, he promises,

> we shall build new castles and a brand-new city,
> there we shall raise new hopes and virtues, joys and sorrows,
> there our strong arms will finish what the proud heart orders.
>
> (XI, 1325–1327)

This is a positive Odysseus. We suspect, though, that this new experiment in social organization will be less beneficent than is implied. The benevolent social motive will be a cloak.

After an enormously difficult trek, during which Hunger and Terror, dramatizations of Odysseus' god, make themselves continually felt, Odysseus and his band reach their destination. There Odysseus, seeking the vision on which to found his new city, climbs to a high mountain (Book XIV) and communes with the "nature of reality," in the hope of founding his city upon it. But what Odysseus discovers there does not soften his relations to society. He finds that reality is a stumbling but bloody and inexorable ascent of god through matter toward spirit. This is no longer the maleficent god of Book XI, who hated mankind. But it is a god who is totally indifferent to the individual, who tolerates humanity only as an artery of his own pounding force. It is this god that Odysseus plans to serve, as he descends from the mountain.

Back in his new community he begins slowly to indoctrinate citizens, and the spirit of the state as a whole, with his severe evolutionary metaphysics. He approaches his "people" as a crafty master. They are divided into three groups—craftsmen, warriors, and intellectuals—whose interrelations are fundamentally communistic: children are to be educated in common, older people allowed to die. Odysseus is impressed when he sees a baby camel devoured by a pack of ants. This particular experience accelerates his intention to bring his city more directly into line with his philosophy. In a number of scenes—a fertility ceremony, a declaration of joy at the death of an old chieftain who had fulfilled his purpose in life—he prepares the people for the truth. He chisels his Ten Commandments into living rock. And then, when it is time to inaugurate the city, nature intervenes, to *prove* the truth of the leader's philosophy. A tremendous earthquake wipes out Odysseus' embodied vision, at the same time confirming his disembodied conviction that even bloody and aborted struggle toward "spirit" is a manifestation of God.

What we see to this point is a slow alienation of Odysseus from warm, familial, social contexts. That alienation is slow, not briskly shown. Yet when we consider the various "social" scenes against which Odysseus plays his character in the first fifteen books—against the backgrounds of family, Helen, his men, and a section of society, in that order—we are impressed by two lines of development: of movement away from the warm, personal, intimate; of movement toward relationships which are increasingly abstract, promoted by the hero's principles. Both of these movements accelerate after Book XV.

From that point on, the only true relation accessible to Odysseus is an inward one, or rather an inward-cosmic one, a relation to the cosmic attained within himself. He will meet many more people, but will fail to encounter them closely; he will seem almost to pass them by, as if in a separate existential compartment. After the destruction of his city he will be mainly concerned to be true to himself—as an ascetic mediator—and, through himself, to the ultimate character of reality. Here is the secret of his successful transcendence of the ego, his ascension to a more than personal level.

The first stage of his spiritual trajectory, "in beyond" other people, away from the social altogether, can be delimited by the period between his first true practice of asceticism (Book XVI) and his encounter with the Negro fisher (Book XXI). In that time, prior to his suicidal departure from South Africa for the South Pole, Odysseus is attempting to define his own convictions more accurately, and to try them in encounters with a group of "exemplary" figures.

In becoming an ascetic, after his experiment with city-planning, Odysseus does not revolt in disgust against a former way of life and thought. Both the content of his thought and the attitude he adopts are continuous with the old. In thought he enlarges his dreadful former evolutionism with a more loving pantheism: this recourse saves him, enabling him to savor the good in nature, even in the midst of destructiveness:

> Odysseus brimmed with waters, trees, fruit, beasts, and snakes
> and all trees, waters, beasts, and fruit brimmed with Odysseus.
>
> (XVI, 476–477)

In the attitude—especially toward the human world—which accompanies this change of thought, Odysseus isolates himself more than before. Growing closer to nonhuman nature, he draws away from the human. Even in his negotiation with the one inescapable feature of the human, himself, he expresses himself as though concerned with a part of outer nature. We see this in his peroration to his five senses (XVI, 489–562). He praises each sense as partially himself, partially the natural outer world with which that sense coincided.

> O ears—he exclaims—O serpent spirals, caves of the rattler's peal
> of many copper bells, remember how you reared
> upright like savage flame to hear what the world rang!
>
> (XVI, 503–505)

Or, to his sense of taste:

> O crimson lips that kissed—and still the kiss remains—
> intoxicating honey, fuzzy peach, and mellow wine,
> how much I love you that with myriad veins and thin
> transparent skin kissed all the world full on the mouth.
>
> (XVI, 516–519)

Odysseus, here, mentions no human lips.

The convictions into which Odysseus is growing are tried out on a number of exemplary characters, characters who are almost allegorical. Of most importance are a prince (Buddha?), a world-famous prostitute, an impractical idealist (Don Quixote?), a hedonist, and a Negro fisher-boy (Christ?).

No longer does Odysseus transact seriously with the human. He no longer looks for, or wants, love. He has no intention, or real hope, of converting or of constructing. He has, as he remarks after the destruction of his city, passed beyond "all sorrow, joy, or love." He enters into dialectic with his allegorical opponents: he reproves the prince for passivity, the hedonist for indifference, and the impractical idealist for idealism; he even reproves the Negro fisher-boy, who alone makes a significant impression on him. It is only in this encounter that

Odysseus feels himself confronted by another philosophy of vital power. This meeting is well conceived. It culminates in Odysseus' test of the boy's philosophy:

> He crept behind the youth, then raised his hand and struck
> the unsuspecting lad hard on his tingling cheek
> as all his friends jumped to their feet with growling rage—
> but the young fisher smiled and turned his other cheek:
> "O white-haired brother, strike again to ease your heart!"
> But the sun-archer's shriveled hand hung down with shame:
> "Forgive me, friend, I longed to measure your strange mind,
> to cast my plumb line and find out what depths you sail.
> The seas you sail are fathomless! O pilot, hail!"
>
> (XXI, 1232–1241)

With the exception of this scene, however, there is almost no felt dialogue between Odysseus and the representative figures who cross his path in these last days of his existence among mortals. His final words to the fisher are meaningful:

> "Farewell! our meeting was most good, and good your words,
> but better still this parting which will last forever."
>
> (XXI, 1364–1365)

Casting off from land in a skiff which he has carved in the form of his coffin, Odysseus leaves for his last encounter, with Death. In the final three books we see him almost entirely isolated from other beings, sailing toward the South Pole. He is no longer thinking and expressing the pantheism which had calmed him after the destruction of his city. To a great degree he now *is* the nature which he had before imagined himself part of. Even the distance of thought has vanished. As he sails interminably through the half-frozen seas, past icebergs, under a still Antarctic sky, he merges into his environment. The spirit of the surrounding world enters him:

> God is wide waterways that branch throughout man's heart
>
> (XXII, 419)

he says, taking the long water channels under him as his own struggling nature. The essential vision of the last three books is of man's inextricable, progressive return into the elemental source.

This hero's last meeting with humanity has less than ever of the human, and indeed ends in natural disaster. Having crashed into an iceberg, Odysseus is thrown onto land, and makes his way—with great difficulty—to an eskimo settlement. There he remains for some time, in the igloo of the witch doctor. Life in the igloo is hard; humanity is there forever besieged by Hunger and Hardship; all thoughts are turned toward Spring. Odysseus, like the others, simply holds on to existence, and endures. Then, when spring comes, the whole community leaves winter quarters for summer fields, and Odysseus accompanies them down to the shore, from which he will once more begin his trip toward the Pole. Sailing out in his kyak, he looks back at the eskimos, only to see them all rush toward, and be swallowed by, a gaping crack in the ice. At first he is horrified, tempted to damn God. His last feeling, though, is praise.

> O soul,—he says—you stretch your bottomless, your unslaked palms
> to quench your endless thirst with that immortal water, Death!
>
> (XXII, 1475–1476)

Such general praise, directed at the general, futile character of the human drama, is the last note of the epic. Odysseus has finally been thrown from his boat, and is dying, trying to hold with bloody hands to the face of an ice cliff. Through his mind—and this is the theme of the last book—pour pell-mell all of his former comrades and friends. All his memories of people fill him. Yet the reunion is unsentimental: it has the supreme calm and distance of an epic summation. All that humanity from whose warmth Odysseus has been gradually separating himself—in favor of closeness to nature—is called up in a fictive last vision, which finds the man for a removed, desperate instant again hospitable to the human.

Spiritual movement and change are central to Kazantzakis' creation. I have allowed, already, for the limitations of this point. The Odysseus of Book I, who meets Telemachus and Penelope, is recognizably the same character who sails to death at the South Pole. In one sense, Odysseus is "unified": his questingness, vitality, and energy are constant. To this degree he resembles Homer's character. Yet within this unity a modern restlessness is held. Odysseus is determined to revise himself, to seek, ceaselessly, and to do so with an alert consciousness of his own directions. Here is the paradox of the literary character who is pre-eminently a quester. His "traits" forever exist in tension, threaten to be displaced. "Character" threatens to dissolve itself.

Homer's Odysseus lacks this kind of inner tension. Organically vigorous, he nevertheless remains essentially static. He is always identical with himself in the limited sense of "standing for" and "displaying" the same moods and thoughts from beginning to end.

This general difference in character may be hastily summarized as that between the "vertical" character (Kazantzakis' Odysseus) and the "horizontal" character (Homer's Odysseus). The vertical character is one whose movement as mind and spirit, though not necessarily as moral being, is "upward." He changes, but, like Kazantzakis' own Odysseus, he does not simply change. For as the plot which involves him develops, growing at every stage more complex, because it subsumes the stages which have preceded it, so the character himself develops, subsumes, and grows more complex.[4] "Change," here, takes on evolutionary significance: it involves the preservation, at each new stage of the character's growth, of all the preceding stages. The "horizontal" character, by contrast, not only remains the same—in the

---

[4] It is worth remembering Kazantzakis' felt affinity to Bergson, with whom he studied at the Collège de France. Bergson's philosophy of time led him (Bergson) to reflect on the subsumptive aspect of every new instant of organic reality. Each moment, each organic entity grows, "changes" through the synthesis of what it has been with what it now is: there is no flat, "additive" development in organisms.

sense proposed above—but he does not grow more complex with the development of his plot. It will be seen, of course, that the application of this point to a character like Homer's Odysseus needs qualification. Still it holds. When we think of Odysseus first on Calypso's island, then before the Phaeacians, and finally on his own island—even *after* he has told us so much about himself in Books IX–XII—we feel in the presence of a character who is not essentially growing more complex. He has been moving horizontally.[5]

This distinction, of course, still leaves us well outside Kazantzakis' craft and vision, in his *Odyssey*. I have not made it clear—if that can be done—just *how* Kazantzakis has managed to remake the Homeric Odysseus into a "vertical" character, just *how* he has been able to dynamize the myth in his way. That question, which leads toward the center of Kazantzakis' re-experience of an ancient theme, is not a preliminary one. We cannot speak of some "handling from the inside" in Kazantzakis, as though Homer had been less adroit at that. Homer was a master of brief speech and significant action which seemed to grow from the essential nature of his characters. We must speak, rather, of a distinctive view and grasp of character in literature, which led Kazantzakis to reconstruct his myth as he did. We may imagine Kazantzakis to have dealt, at the initiatory stages of the work on his *Odyssey,* not with a theme which was public property and which could properly be perfected as such, but—given the mind of our age and the long seasoning of the myth—with a gradually shaping inner vision full of "intentions" and "implications" meaningful to him. These intentions—senses of the clash between spirit and matter, of some kind of transcendence through spirit, of the superiority of quest over discovery, and so forth—found their way into a whole verbal product, a verbal

---

[5] The issue for literary theory—in this distinction of types of character—is important. The problem does not reduce to that of the "flat" vs. the "round" character—E. M. Forster's distinction—but to that of different kinds of "round" character.

unity of feeling, Odysseus. We will not imagine that any doctrinaire view of the literary character led Kazantzakis to this kind of creation. It will have been the case, simply, that certain potentialities, above all certain preoccupations with transcendence and growth, in his own character, translated themselves into Odysseus. Homer's Odysseus could hardly have been re-encountered on a deeper subjective level.[6]

[6] For a different way of looking at the epic—particularly in terms of the dramatized quest for *freedom*—cf. George Scouffas, "Kazantzakis: Odysseus and the 'Cage of Freedom'," *Accent* (Autumn, 1959), pp. 234–246.

THE EMBATTLED MYTHS

By Leon S. Roudiez

THE LEGENDS of ancient Greece, in one way or another, have found themselves in the thick of literary controversy ever since they were restored, so to speak, by Renaissance humanists. Not too surprisingly, they have managed to survive the various melees and are still with us today. Just as important as their survival, however, is the manner in which they have been involved in the battles—the fact that throughout the centuries men have been probing deeper and deeper into their meaning.

The famous seventeenth-century *Querelle* was, from our point of view, a mere skirmish. While Perrault and the moderns won—and their victory was significant in view of the rising age of enlightenment—the ancient myths were involved only superficially, caught as they were in the gestation of a theory of progress. But the writers of the eighteenth century did not, as a rule, turn their backs on the Greek legends. This, one suspects, is because they, like their seventeenth-century predecessors, too often viewed them as convenient, well-known parables, or stories, or even mere embellishments.

The enmity of Chateaubriand was more meaningful. His praise and use of Christian imagery as opposed to classical mythology linked the "ornaments" of literature to the writer's outlook on life; in stressing the appropriateness of Biblical themes in a Catholic culture he also pointed to what separated them from the pagan myths—thus unwittingly reinforcing the moral significance of all myths, whatever their source. Even though Chateaubriand's example was followed, in France, by any number of romantic writers, the Parnassians were not far behind. The latter, as some critics have suggested, may not always have been able to distinguish Alexandria from Athens, but their coming coincided more or less with the disintegration of Christian religious belief. This in turn opened the way to a freer interpretation of Christian—or medieval— myths: in the past, a poet who handled Christian myths continuously courted the dangers of heresy or blasphemy. Even when those pitfalls were avoided, a pious reader might occasionally look at the whole enterprise as profanation of sacred texts. The liberation from orthodoxy enjoyed by the Christian myths reactivated the power that was theirs during the Middle Ages and undoubtedly encouraged writers to view all myths with a fresher and bolder spirit.

In our post-Nietzschean world both Greek and non-Greek fountain-heads of myth are thus competing on the basis of the fundamental viewpoints inherent in their conception. It is hardly surprising that the surrealists, for instance, should mostly disregard the Greeks. One member of their group, Julien Gracq, following the lead of many romantic authors, has revived several medieval myths, but he has divested them of their Christian flavor. A recent critic, in sympathy with the goals of surrealism, has ascribed classical allusions to a lack of imagination and gone so far as to write that "the myth of Sisyphus is obsolete."[1] This does not alter the fact that, along with the near-surrealist Jean Cocteau, some of the major French writers of this century, who do not always lack imagination, have made continuous appeals to Greek mythical figures—including Sisyphus.[2]

[1] Anna Balakian, *Surrealism: The Road to the Absolute* (New York, 1959), p. 200.

[2] Cf. Gilbert Highet, *The Classical Tradition* (New York, 1949), Chapter 23.

It is true that many twentieth-century thinkers have endeavored to cut themselves loose from the moorings their predecessors had imagined to be safe and permanent, and they are now in search of a past as well as a future, a justification, and even an identity. Disillusioned with the more artificial concepts of our civilization, they seek out the roots of being, exploring dark recesses that had hitherto been carefully concealed. In France such literary explorers as have concentrated their creative efforts in the field of the novel are known as the practitioners of *le roman nouveau*. The members of this vastly heterogeneous group (Robbe-Grillet, Butor, Sarraute, Simon, et al.) actually have little more in common than a strong distaste for conventional literature, for the traditional forms and techniques of the novel: some of their own works have occasionally been called "antinovels." They might have been expected to display equal scorn for the "traditional" myths; but this is another instance where no generalization or logical presupposition will account for all individual practices.

Certainly Alain Robbe-Grillet, who was for a time regarded as the spokesman for the *roman nouveau* group—until it was realized that the group was merely a figment of critics' imaginations—was the most unlikely one to resort to Greek myth. Indeed, in one of his essays he specifically denounced those humanistic and tragic concepts the reader almost immediately identifies with what he believes is the Greek view of life;[3] furthermore, Robbe-Grillet has also rejected symbolic or mythical interpretations of reality: in his view the world has no particular meaning—and that very statement is of no particular import. Things are as they are, and that is all there is to it. This brings to mind the contemporary interpretation of Greek thought that, refusing to see it through the eyes of Aristotle and Plato, denies any ethical or even "tragic" significance to the great tragedies. As Henry Bamford Parkes put it a few years ago, the "essentially Philistine conception, which

[3] Alain Robbe-Grillet, "Nature, humanisme, tragédie," *Nouvelle Revue Française*, VI (October, 1958), 580–604.

implies that suffering is a punishment for sin, does not apply to a single
Greek tragedy, not even those of Sophocles. Oedipus and Antigone do
not suffer because of any flaw or error but because life is like that." [4]
Without debating the merits of this case, it seems clear that the
anti-Greek attitude of Robbe-Grillet bears a striking resemblance to the
views attributed by Mr. Parkes to the Greeks of Homeric and classical
ages. The irony of the situation is that, although Robbe-Grillet
obviously shares the more common, romantic view of Greek literature,
simply assuming that the other interpretation is truer to fact, he finds
himself in the position of attacking Greek myths in order to re-
establish what amounts to a classical Greek outlook on life. And the fact
remains that in his first novel at least, he consciously and pointedly
makes use of a tragic Greek myth. I now propose to examine that novel,
Les Gommes, showing the peculiar part played in it by myth, and then
to confront it with the novel by Michel Butor called *L'Emploi du
temps.*[5]

Robbe-Grillet and Butor, contrary to the practice of French writers of
the previous generations, do not retell a mythical story, adding or
subtracting an episode, modifying or suppressing a character. Much
more in the manner of James Joyce, both use the myth as a backdrop for
a contemporary plot that seems to have no direct connection to the older
legend. Unlike *Ulysses,* however, the titles of their novels give no hint as
to what might be forthcoming. On the other hand, while conspicuous
references to the *Odyssey* have been removed from the final version of
Joyce's work, the reader of *Les Gommes* and *L'Emploi du temps,*
throughout those novels, is handed a number of more or less transparent

[4] Henry Bamford Parkes, "Homer and Hellenism," *Partisan Review,* XXI
(September–October, 1954), 563 n.

[5] Alain Robbe-Grillet, *Les Gommes* (Paris, 1953); Michel Butor, *L'Emploi du
temps* (Paris, 1957). So far, *Les Gommes* has not been published in English, but a
translation by Richard Howard is scheduled for 1964; a translation of *L'Emploi
du temps* was published in 1960 and given the distressingly frivolous title, *Passing
Time.* In either case, references to the French editions will appear in the text, and
the translations are my own.

clues so that the author's intent will not be lost: in the background of Robbe-Grillet's story looms the myth of Oedipus; in the background of Butor's, mainly that of Theseus.

On the surface, *Les Gommes* reads very much like a mystery novel: a crime seems to have been committed in a small provincial city, and a detective is sent from Paris to investigate what is generally thought to have been a murder; the victim, however, had only been wounded and he comes out of hiding just in time to be killed by the detective who has mistaken him for the criminal. A vast web of politically subversive organizations, hidden economic influences on governmental policies, and competing police agencies quite conventionally add to the expected confusion and suspense. But that, of course, is not the main point: Robbe-Grillet is no more interested in relating a murder story than the Greeks were interested in dealing with the murder of Laius per se. His main concern is with the interpretation of reality: he shows the reader what the reality is and how it is interpreted by the various characters; enough information is then provided for him to interpret the novel—or misinterpret it if he is not careful.

The detective, as he wanders through the provincial town, seeking to clear up the mystery surrounding the murder (very few characters know that it was only an attempted murder) of a professor of economics, is also trying to buy an eraser of a certain make—the name of which he has forgotten. The erasers ("les gommes") give the novel its theme as well as its title. The one he is attempting to duplicate still bears part of the trade name on its side: the letters "di" remain, and it is apparent that originally two letters preceded and two letters followed. Of course, any number of French names would fit, "Didier" for instance; and, no doubt, one such name originally did appear on the eraser. But, by means of other allusions that I shall discuss presently, Robbe-Grillet forces one solution upon the reader's mind—the Gallicized name "Œdipe." What Robbe-Grillet wishes to erase are the centuries-old myths and prejudices that falsify our vision of reality: he thinks we have been so thoroughly conditioned by the heritage of our Western culture that we automatically interpret events by means of that cultural key. Even "the least conditioned observer does not succeed in seeing the world about him with free eyes." [6] Quite literally then, Robbe-Grillet will have us erase the myth from our consciousness; he will do this by means of an instrument bearing a trade name that our prejudices make us believe to be that of Oedipus. Translated over to the level of the plot, the novelist will deny mythical interpretations by means of fragmentary references to what our cultural background assures us is the myth of Oedipus—a myth that constantly is popping into the story and confusing the issue. Thus, as the detective asks for his eraser in a store and the merchant inquires as to what kind of an eraser he wants, the author comments: "That is precisely the whole story" (p. 122). Oedipus or Didier? If we choose Oedipus we embark on a myth-chasing venture, and, like the detective, we are sure to end up in failure.

That the references to the story of Oedipus represent a distortion of the plot's reality is made clear by the author in at least two specific instances. First, we are shown an elderly passer-by reading a political poster on a school wall (schools, by the way, are the artificial agencies through which myths now come down to us); after he has finished and he starts on his way again, he is quite puzzled, for he wonders if he hasn't missed the main point of the poster: "In the midst of the usual words there emerges here and there, like a beacon, a suspicious term—and the sentence it illuminates in a strange fashion seems for a moment to conceal many things, or perhaps nothing at all" (p. 42). This is no more than an ambiguous reminder of what Robbe-Grillet had said elsewhere: "All about us, defying the pack of our animalistic or house-broken adjectives, things *are there*. Their surface is clean and smooth, *intact,* but without any strange luminosity or transparency." [7]

[6] Alain Robbe-Grillet, "Une Voie pour le roman futur," *Nouvelle Revue Française* (July, 1956), 80.
[7] *Ibid.,* p. 81.

The references to Oedipus are of course the suspicious terms that show the story of *Les Gommes* in a very peculiar light, giving it that "strange luminosity" we have been conditioned to expect.

Secondly, later in the novel, the detective happens by a stationery store that also sells artists' supplies. One of the store windows displays an enlarged photographic reproduction of the house where the "crime" has been committed; in front of it, as if he were confronting reality, a dummy dressed up as a painter is seated by an easel and is contemplating the landscape representation he has supposedly painted. But what we see on the canvas is a Greek landscape with cypress trees, the ruins of a temple, and an ancient city in the background—obviously Thebes. As Robbe-Grillet points out, the realistic qualities of the photograph are brought out most strikingly because the picture negates the canvas that was supposed to reproduce it (p. 121). The implication seems clear: the myth of Oedipus is negated by the plot of *Les Gommes*. More generally, myth fails as an attempt to explain reality and is denied by reality.

Leaving aside for a moment all the seemingly explicit references to the story of Oedipus that have been inserted into the novel, the actual resemblances between *Les Gommes* and the outline of the Greek myth as it has come down to us are limited to the following: a relatively young man, who has recently changed his allegiance, is doggedly attempting to solve a mystery involving, he believes, the murder of an older man; in spite of incongruous warnings that point to the similarities between the supposed murderer and himself, and in spite of having his search apparently hampered or perhaps directed by Fate, he sticks to his task until the moment he is revealed as the killer of the older man—and must change his allegiance again.

That may not be quite enough for the cultured reader to decide that *Les Gommes* is a symbolic novel and that the myth of Oedipus will reveal its hidden significance. But Robbe-Grillet has maliciously inserted those previously-mentioned "beacons" which, like the songs of the Sirens, are intended to charm the reader and shipwreck him on a dangerous island of myth. Thus, on the opening pages of the novel, he is confronted with a sphinxlike drunk who annoys patrons of the *café* where the detective has taken a room by asking a series of insoluble riddles (the drunk also claims to have been nearly killed by the detective); with flotsam fortuitously assembling in the water of a canal and forming the image of a fabulous creature with the body of a lion and wings of an eagle; with the detective's remembering having been in the town when he was a small child; with a motif on a curtain representing shepherds caring for an abandoned child; with the fact that a gynecologist, involved in the plot, lives on Corinth Street; with a sculpture of the Chariot of State, which might well be that of Laius; with the reappearance of the drunk, who now is a Tiresias-like seer; with the local post office's assuming appearances of the Temple at Delphi—full of secret rules, multiple rites, and sibylline writing; with a figurine representing a blind man guided by a child; with the news that the victim had a son who has disappeared; with the fact that the detective, whose feet at one point are said to be swollen, seems attracted to the wife of the victim; and with a series of murders that have hit the country like an epidemic: it is the detective's task to bring this plague to an end.

That all these elements are false leads that have absolutely no bearing on the plot of the novel is also made clear, although perhaps less obviously. The drunk is a mere nuisance; his sphinxlike riddles are not solved by the detective, nor is he killed by him; his Tiresias-like utterances are meaningless. The flotsam, after figuring a sphinx, reassembles to form the image of the American continent; all one needs, in order to see such images, is "de la bonne volonté" (p. 27). The detective came to the town as a child in order to visit his father; he did not originate there. Mythological scenes are found in pictorial or sculptured representations all over the Western world and do not help interpret contemporary events taking place in their vicinity. The gynecologist has the reputation of being an abortionist, rather than a

provider for abandoned children. The detective learns nothing from
questioning the post office employees. The story concerning the victim's
son, who is supposed to have been illegitimate anyway, is shown to have
materialized only because of the zeal, imagination, and leading questions
of a young police investigator. The detective neither seduces nor marries
the victim's estranged wife—who is no more his mother than the victim
is his father. The epidemic of murders goes on even as the detective
emerges as killer. The latter's swollen feet cannot be traced back to any
childhood experience but rather to his having walked too much during
the twenty-four hours covered by his search. Finally, his act does not
make him a criminal—it is merely a blunder, an unfortunate accident,
and the detective will be, of his own accord, transferred back to another
department.

Further emphasizing Robbe-Grillet's message, most of the characters
in the novel are mythomaniacs of one sort or another, and each in his
own way makes the solution of the puzzling pseudo murder more
difficult to arrive at. Aside from the detective, who is little more than a
passive, bungling pawn, the most conspicuous exception is the local
police commissioner: impervious to the fantasies conjured by the minds
of subordinates and strangers as well, he is completely at home with the
realities of his town. It is he who, putting to a rational test all possible
hypotheses, arrives, unaided, at the correct solution of the original
mystery—too late, however, to prevent the detective from committing
his homicidal error.

The detective, then, stands for contemporary man who fails to
question his heritage of myths and is unable to see reality with a "free
vision." It is thus one of the ironies of this antimythical novel that it
does contain a number of symbols. In addition to the detective and his
erasers, there is the detective's watch, which mysteriously stops at 7:30
P.M., time of the attempted murder, and just as unaccountably starts
again at 7:30 P.M. on the following day when he kills the man whose
"murder" he was attempting to solve. It is during that timeless episode

that everything has taken place: fantasy has displaced reality, the unwitting agent of myth has taken over; before and after, the realistic police commissioner is in charge. Those unreal twenty-four hours, the only hours that can belong to the "timeless" myths, are truly superfluous and harmful hours: such appears to be the point of Robbe-Grillet's ironic and didactic book.[8]

If this indeed be the correct interpretation of *Les Gommes,* one cannot help feeling that Robbe-Grillet is wrong. Not so much because of his possible misinterpretation of the Greek view of tragedy, for this enters the novel only indirectly; rather for his denial that myths have a meaning in the contemporary world and for the kind of meaning he seems to discuss.

A very different, if not antithetical, approach is illustrated by Michel Butor. Published four years after *Les Gommes,* his *Emploi du temps* reads almost like a refutation of Robbe-Grillet's first novel. His title is descriptive, rather than symbolic. Like *Les Gommes* it is divided into five parts, suggestive of neoclassical tragedy; but it lacks Robbe-Grillet's prologue and conclusion: in other words, the intricacies of the plot are not presented as a fantastic spectacle, framed by reality, but as reality itself. Allusions to Greek myths are suggestive and meaningful rather than ironic and destructive: Butor, although he is an admirer of the surrealist André Breton, fully accepts what I have called the romantic view of Greek legends and adds to them in turn.

Les Gommes was told through the conventional device of the omniscient author; *L'Emploi du temps* appears in the form of a diary through which a Frenchman is attempting to account for the time he has spent (and is still spending while the "novel" is taking shape) in an

---

[8] Since this essay was written, two book-length studies on Robbe-Grillet have appeared. Bruce Morrissette, in *Les Romans de Robbe-Grillet* (Paris: Editions de Minuit, 1963), disagrees with my interpretation of *Les Gommes;* Olga Bernal, in *Alain Robbe-Grillet: Le Roman de l'absence* (Paris: Gallimard, 1964) has independently arrived at conclusions similar to mine.

English city where he has contracted to work for a year as a clerk with a local firm. As he unsuccessfully tries to gain an authentic consciousness of time and of the events it contains, he becomes involved in two abortive love affairs and in the complicated ramifications of a mystery story he has read; he is also concerned with an accident that could have been an attempted murder, and with a series of fires some of which involve arson. Eventually, as the year comes to an end, he is a defeated man leaving a dying city.

The outline of the plot is even less suggestive of the Theseus story than the outline of *Les Gommes* is of the Oedipus myth. But Butor is not attempting to give another account of the adventures of Theseus, nor is he making use of that legend alone. Typical of his acceptance of the whole background of Western culture is his setting up as symbolic foci of the novel two buildings that correspond to the Greek and the Biblical fountainheads of our myths: the Museum of Fine Arts and the Old Cathedral. (To complicate matters there is also an important New Cathedral, and I shall touch upon its role very briefly.) The Old Cathedral's main feature, for the purposes of the plot, is a stained-glass window depicting Cain's murder of Abel; the Museum's is a five-room sequence (as many as there are parts in the novel) where eighteen tapestries are hung—each representing an episode from the story of Theseus. (Even though an elucidation of all mythical references would be necessary for a full comprehension of the novel, I shall deal with the myth of Cain only to the extent that it is interwoven with that of Theseus.)

Butor does not scatter allusions to the Greek myth haphazardly and teasingly throughout the novel: he introduces them gradually and in such a manner that the reader is almost subconsciously ready for the myth when it is specifically mentioned. (Not once does Robbe-Grillet actually spell out the name of Oedipus in *Les Gommes*.) Jacques Revel, the narrator of *L'Emploi du temps*, attempting to familiarize himself with his strange surroundings, purchases a map of the city of Bleston.

That evening, he spreads the map on his bed and remarks: "Now I, a mole bumping at every step against its mud corridors, . . . I have taken in the whole expanse of the city at a glance" (p. 43). The allusion is a subtle one that might easily be overlooked. Standing alone, it would, of course, be meaningless. A few pages later, however, Revel throws in a key word: describing his activities over a week end, he tells about going for a walk in Lanes Park "which features a small labyrinth . . ." (p. 49). Slowly, assisted by Revel's account of his wanderings in the town, Bleston and the labyrinth become linked in the reader's mind. Much later he discovers that the labyrinth is not only a symbol of Bleston, i.e., of the world in which we find ourselves, but also of the narrator's consciousness: "The thread of sentences that is being coiled up in this pile [the sheaf of papers on which he has been writing his diary] . . . is the thread of Ariadne, because I am writing in order to find my way . . ." (p. 187).

The same technique is used to introduce another key word. Having been invited to the home of one of his fellow employees, Revel notices, among other things, two pictures on the wall, one representing "some deposed king or other, fleeing, draped in his cloak, his crown on his head, . . ." (p. 52). When he visits the Museum he sees the tapestries depicting a late version of the Theseus story; but, like the reader who still may not suspect that there is a connection between the stories of Revel and Theseus, he does not identify the scenes at his first visit, for they are not labeled (p. 70). The tapestries are reported to be an eighteenth-century work commissioned from Beauvais by a fictitious Duke of Harrey; the last of the panels represents Theseus in exile and the city of Athens burning in the distance. Thus Bleston, because of its fires, is not only the labyrinth in Crete, but also Athens—the kingdom of Theseus. One might recall at this point that the name of Athens is thought to signify "the whole enclosure of the Old and New Town," [9] just as Bleston comprised the Old and New Cathedrals.

[9] Charles Anthon, "A Classical Dictionary" (New York, 1865), p. 1328.

In the meantime, a similar process has gradually imposed Cain upon the reader's consciousness and, after visiting the Museum, Revel goes to the Old Cathedral to look at the stained-glass windows. There he sees "Cain killing his brother Abel, Cain clad in armor tightly fitted around his midriff with ribbons streaming about his thighs like Theseus, almost in the same attitude as Theseus struggling with the Minotaur, . . ." (p. 72). We now begin to have a clearer notion of what Butor is doing: he is not telling a story according to a traditional pattern, or reinterpreting a myth as Gide had done for the same Theseus legend. He is drawing upon the latent suggestive powers of myth to spark the imagination of his reader and thus enrich the significance of the narrative. We are not presented with a double equation, Revel=Theseus=Cain; rather, we are invited to lean on the universal meaning of the Theseus and Cain myths in order to generalize the individual experience of Revel—that is, of Butor himself. The latter, a careful reader of James Joyce and of Joyce criticism, and who has also read Vico, is much closer, in his handling of mythical material, to the author of *Ulysses* than to Gide, Sartre, Anouilh, or Giraudoux—much closer, too, than Robbe-Grillet.

That the myth basically belongs in the background is shown when Revel goes to a movie theater to see a travelogue on Crete. Long lyrical paragraphs stress the differences between Bleston and Crete: "How clear are the days in that country, on the slopes of Mount Ida . . . How clear the days over the orange groves . . ." (p. 101). He also notes that the view of Crete given by the travelogue differs considerably from that depicted on the Museum tapestries. Butor is agreeing here that the Greeks' experience of life was different from our own; that their myths were undoubtedly told in more simple fashion; that they interpreted them in their own special way; that the artist who executed the tapestries also had his own outlook on life, his own way of depicting the myth and his own interpretation of it. No matter how much we attempt to recapture the Greek spirit, their myths can no longer mean the same to us, living in different surroundings and beset with different problems. That is not to say, however, as implied by Robbe-Grillet, that they have lost all meaning.

On the contrary, they have, if anything, acquired new meaning. Our concept of them stands in relation to the Greeks' as the New Cathedral of Bleston stands to the Old: ". . . there was in that strange structure much more than a rehash, it had indeed been impressed upon me that an extraordinarily bold mind had violently distorted the traditional themes, ornaments, and details, thus achieving a work that is certainly imperfect, I am tempted to say lacking, but filled nevertheless, with a deep, irrefutable dream, a secret germinating power, a pathetic call to freer and better results. . . . how precious was that distortion!" (pp. 121–122). From a strict classicist's point of view, Butor's—and more generally the contemporary writers'—interpretation of Greek myth is distorted indeed; but it has been enriched by centuries of accumulated experience.

To return to the narrative of *L'Emploi du temps,* Revel is a civilized man in quest of his identity. The search he makes in his immediate, individual past is symbolic of the more general search of modern man's consciousness. There is thus poetic logic in Butor's calling upon Cain and Theseus to illuminate his problem: both were founders of cities and, consequently, fathers of civilized man. Contemporary man, however, has embarked on his quest because he feels alienated in the midst of his own civilization and finds himself at odds with it. Even though his aim is constructive he turns out to be destructive in pursuing it and he unwittingly undermines the civilization that has fathered him. As Theseus, in one version of the myth, sets fire to the Labyrinth after killing the Minotaur, so does Revel symbolically set fire to Bleston by burning the map of the city—and this fire is echoed throughout the book by real fires that constantly and inexplicably break out in various parts of town. The hostility displayed by Revel toward his "kingdom," Bleston (the name is said to have been derived from *Belli Civitas*), like that displayed by twentieth-century writers toward their environment, is partly what determines his eventual failure.

Other characters also reinforce the Theseus legend. Early in the novel, Revel meets two sisters, Ann and Rose Bailey, one of whom provides him with the "thread," i.e., a map so that he will find his way within himself. Allusions to the love affairs of Theseus are "distorted"—to use Butor's word—by their being commingled with the quest motif and its related theme of courtship. As Revel successively courts one sister and the other and loses them both, just as Theseus, although in a different manner, also lost both daughters of Minos, Butor enlarges upon the original myth. As Revel shows the Museum tapestries to Lucien, a young Frenchman more recently arrived in Bleston, he muses: ". . . for me henceforth Ariadne stood for Ann Bailey, . . . Phaedra stood for Rose, . . . I myself was Theseus, . . . [Lucien] was that young Prince whom, on the fifteenth panel—the descent into Hades—, I guided toward the conquest of Pluto's wife, the queen of the realm of the dead—Proserpina." He then added, "I recognize him now not only as Pirithous . . . but also as this other figure . . . this god, this Dionysus of the twelfth panel, landing on Naxos . . ." (p. 173). Like Revel, secondary characters assume more than one mythical relation, thus reflecting the ambiguity of their situation. Rose, for instance, assumes two Greek and one medieval identity as her relationship with Revel changes: "Rose, my Persephone, my Phaedra, my Rose . . . alas, not at all my Rose, but only Rose, the forbidden Rose, . . ." (p. 208).

In addition to his other concerns, Revel is induced to seek the solution to a peculiar Bleston puzzle. The brother of one Richard Tenn has died—accidentally, it seems. Subsequently there appears a mystery novel, *The Bleston Murder,* dealing with the killing, by his own brother, of a cricket player named Johnny Winn. Striking similarities between the home of the murderer, as described in the novel, and the actual home of Richard Tenn, lead Revel to wondering if *The Bleston Murder* is not in effect an accusation of murder brought against

Tenn—the more so since the novel was published under a pseudonym. As a consequence, he will now assume the part of the detective (who, in the mystery story, had succeeded in bringing down the murderer) and attempt to unravel the supposed mystery involving Richard Tenn. His quest for identity is thus augmented by the search for a culprit—and we are now reminded of Oedipus. The connection is confirmed when Butor points out that a detective "solves an enigma, . . . kills the one to whom he owes his title, the one without whom he would not exist as such" and that "this murder has been foretold from birth, or, if you prefer, it is part of his nature . . ." (p. 148). We are also reminded of Oedipus when, facing the failure of his attempts, Revel expresses a desire to "burn out my eyes" (p. 252). As we participate in Revel's efforts to reconstruct his past, Butor specifically suggests that Oedipus as well as Theseus should be on our minds. As Revel pauses in front of the seventeenth panel of the tapestry, the one showing the meeting between the Kings of Thebes and of Athens, he reflects on what he calls the inevitability of that meeting: "How many similarities indeed bring together the fates of these two children, deceived as to their births and their race, brought up far from their native cities, both killing the monsters that infested the approaches to those cities, both solving enigmas, freeing the way, both murderers of their fathers . . . both thus obtaining a precarious kingdom, both finally expelled from the throne, watching the burning of their cities, dying away from them, unable to bring them help" (pp. 173–174). Such is in reality the fate of every man, as seen through the experience of Revel and his assumption of the combined and modified legends of Oedipus and Theseus—and the story of Cain as well. (Two brief allusions also show him as a wishful Daedalus and a fleeting Odysseus.)

Revel has carelessly revealed the identity of George William Burton, author of *The Bleston Murder,* and is thus, he fears, indirectly responsible for what very much looks like an attempt on Burton's life. This again brings us back to the legend of Theseus and *his* carelessness;

it also emphasizes a special relationship, intellectual rather than physical, that exists between Revel and Burton (whose name is very nearly an anagram of Butor). As Butor brings his novel to a close, however, nothing is solved: the identity of Burton's intentional or unintentional assailant is in doubt—both Burton's and Tenn's brother's accidents must still be called accidents. As in the novel of Robbe-Grillet, the myths have been of no avail.

But that seems to be precisely the point of Butor's refutation. In the first place, it should be remembered that the solution of those puzzling accidents is not, like the solution of the "murder" in *Les Gommes,* central to the plot. In the second place, myths and fiction are not ciphers that can be used to explain isolated occurrences in the manner that dream-symbols were used by Freud to elucidate individual dreams: in this respect *The Bleston Murder,* a contemporary piece of fiction, is just as much a failure as the ancient myth of Oedipus. Rather, myths are part of an inescapable heritage that, instead of dwindling as it is broken up by successive generations, is being constantly enriched and added to—not only in time but in space. The myth of Theseus, or any other Greek myth for that matter, does not come down to us as it was known or codified at a given moment in Hellenic history; it is the original myth plus what has been added or distorted by other people in other places at different times: myths are "forms that have come down from Athens through Rome, then France, changing shape and aroma at each port of call, . . ." (p. 267). Such transformations result not only from accumulated, but also from variegated experience: myths of diverse cultures have converged on Western civilization and have been assimilated along with Greek myths. This is not a matter of choice: ours is a Judeo-Christian *and* a Hellenic culture. Again on the level of Butor's novel, the legend of Cain also informs the whole story and suggests that Revel-Theseus, as he destroys Bleston, labyrinth, and Minotaur, whose blood-stained muzzle he could feel blowing at him in the night (p. 255), is also a fratricide: for the labyrinth was within himself, too, just as he was part of Bleston and its civilization—and the monster he may well have killed is his soul.

We have come a long way from the superficial arguments of Charles Perrault and his contemporaries. There is, however, some irony and poetic justice in the fact that Vico, forty years younger than Perrault and decidedly a "modern" philosopher, who provided the inspiration for Joyce's last work, is quoted and paraphrased by Butor, whose own interpretation of myth he certainly influenced. In our uncharted journey through time, we cannot, as I interpret Butor, divest our actions and our surroundings of that strange luminosity Robbe-Grillet would deny and which has its source in corresponding deeds and places of the past. The vastness of space echoes back and forth with a series of subdued but sympathetic vibrations: "Thus, each day, arousing other harmonic days, transforms the appearance of the past, and this coming into light of certain areas is generally accompanied by the darkening of others that were once in the light and which become foreign and mute until, after the passage of time, other echoes come to awaken them anew" (p. 294). It is through the resonant myths that a sensitive man enlarges and deepens his perception of the universe. Conversely, as Butor wrote in an essay on Faulkner, "He who is cut off from his own origins, who can gain no information about them, who knows nothing of what has led him to the situation in which he finds himself, cannot reach an awareness of self." [10]

[10] Michel Butor, *Répertoire* (Paris, 1960), p. 251.

POUND AND PROPERTIUS

Some Techniques of Translation

By J. P. Sullivan

W ITH SOME JUSTICE it has been said that the classics can exist only in translation, and perhaps no twentieth-century work illustrates this quite so clearly as Ezra Pound's *Homage to Sextus Propertius*. The understanding and appreciation of Pound's "translation" was a long and painful critical process, and the sneers of classical scholars such as Hale and of imperceptive critics such as Logan Pearsall Smith obfuscated for a long time the true nature of Pound's achievement. Great translations such as Johnson's *Vanity of Human Wishes* and Pope's *Iliad,* and I would class Pound's *Homage* among these, are rare events in an age, but only through them can a dead poetical tradition be brought to life and grafted on to a living poetic tradition. Such translations are rightly termed "creative," for they are not only a fusion of two creative minds, but an enrichment and development of one poetic tradition by means of another.

Each such translation has to have its own poetic strategy and the very inimitability of such translations, which spring from a profound inner solicitation in the poet-translator rather than from some publisher's commission, entails a full utilization of the poet's resources and the techniques of contemporary verse. Pound took Propertius' work and so completely did he "make it new" that the ancient poet was transfigured—in fact, for some he was unrecognizable. From an obscure Roman love poet, popularly estimated as crabbed and difficult, a poet of violent and abrupt transitions, Propertius became, as it were, a modern, and the higher Propertian criticism has not been the same since.

The purpose of this paper is to examine some of the techniques whereby Pound affected this minor revolution in criticism and translation.[1]

Translation is important to Pound because of the very nature of his own poetry. R. P. Blackmur has said that Pound is at his best when he is using another poet to express his own feelings and ideas. It might be more just, however, to say that Pound often realized that what he wanted to express could be expressed only in that particular way, and Pound was prepared to use, as the *Cantos* clearly show, the whole range of literature as the source of his poetic material. Part and parcel of this is his theory of personae, masks of a poetic personality, which serve to widen and deepen that personality:

In the "search for oneself," in the search for "sincere self-expression," one gropes, one finds, for some seeming verity. One says "I am" this, that or the other, and with the words scarcely uttered one ceases to be that thing . . . I began this search for the real in a book called *Personae,* casting off, as it were, complete masks of the self in each poem. I continued in a long series of translations, which were but more elaborate masks.[2]

At a certain period in his development Propertius became one such mask, and we are fortunate in having from Pound himself a brief sketch of the place of the *Homage* in his poetic career. In a letter he said in defense of his poem:

. . . I may perhaps avoid charges of further mystification and obscurity by saying that it [the *Homage*] presents certain emotions as vital to men faced

---

[1] For of course Pound's methods eventually had their imitators. Robert Lowell's *The Ghost: After Sextus Propertius,* for instance, clearly owes something to Pound's example.

[2] Ezra Pound, *Gaudier-Brzeska: A Memoir* (London and New York, John Lane, 1916), p. 98.

with the infinite and ineffable imbecility of the Roman Empire. These emotions are given largely, but not entirely, in Propertius' own terms. If the reader does not find relation to life defined in the poem, he may conclude that I have been unsuccessful in my endeavor . . .[3]

Pound's state of mind in a milieu which hysterically sentimentalized that most idiotic and tragic of human affairs, the First World War, is more clearly seen in *Mauberley* (in this sense at least *Mauberley* is a popularization of the *Homage*). However, it was the Roman poet who became earlier the mask through which Pound registered his protest at what he thought was the monstrous state of society and culture in which he found himself living. Pound's literary flair made him see in Propertius a structure from which he could evolve for his own feelings at the time an artistic credo and an expression of that creed. It was in the ability to absorb that part of Propertius' work and by means of some novel techniques make the Roman elegist his persona that Pound's originality in writing the *Homage* consists. *Mauberley* is a more complex expression of his feelings and it is more intensely charged with emotion, but it is a continuation of the Propertian themes, a clarification of their attitudes—in particular a change from an attitude of resignation and isolation to disgust and despair.

All this naturally affected Pound's view of Propertius. Once he had seen in Propertius (rightly or wrongly) a kindred spirit, his aim was to use him as his mouthpiece. And it is this which gave Pound his positive attitude to Propertius and decided the order of importance he imposed on Propertius' themes. The whole structure and articulation of the *Homage* as a poem depends on Pound's view of Propertius as an alter ego.

Propertius for us is a love poet, but Pound deliberately chose the opening of Book III to begin the *Homage:* Section I discusses the nature of the art of Propertius and the expectations of the artist in a given

---

[3] *The Collected Letters of Ezra Pound,* edited by D. D. Paige (London, Faber & Faber, 1951), pp. 310–311. The letter is to Iris Barry.

society. It is the avowal of the artist's devotion to art and not to public propaganda, even though his audience is thereby limited to "young ladies of indeterminate character" and posterity. *Mauberley* puts it more savagely:

> The age demanded an image
> Of its accelerated grimace . . .
> Not, not certainly, the obscure reveries
> Of the inward gaze . . .

This is also the subject of Sections II and V in a rather different form. In Section II the poet seems about to attempt the very themes he has declared himself unwilling to attempt, but he is recalled from them by Apollo. In Section V he makes another assault on these themes, but the irony and the doubt which pervade the first part of this section

> If I have not the faculty, "The bare attempt would be
> praiseworthy. . . ."

is underlined by the juxtaposition of Part 2:

> Yet you ask on what account I write so many love-lyrics . . .
> My ventricles do not palpitate to Caesarial *ore rotundos*.

This stress on the relation of the artist to society, the vindication of private poetic morality against public compulsions whether these be the demands of a government or promises of fame and fortune, is what Pound saw as the important element in Propertius, and this is the critical burden of the *Homage*.

Propertius' private themes, the center of his art, are in modern eyes love, passion, and his mistress Cynthia; this was his "cultivation of Pierian roses." Here he differs from Pound in the *Homage:* Pound's prime concern is art and artistic freedom. Nevertheless, Pound offers a selection, reworked in a sophisticated manner, of some of the best of the Propertian love elegies. Although there are important other themes, these largely take up Sections III, IV, VI and XI and part of Section

XII, for the subject Propertius has chosen and vindicated against grosser external claims on his poetic allegiance is his love of Cynthia. Pound's allegiances which his persona in *Mauberley* vindicates against the temptations of Mr. Nixon are different, but he is at one with Propertius in the determination to cling to his chosen art. Consequently, although page for page we have more of Propertius' love poetry than his poetic credo, the significance of Propertius for Pound (which he clearly brings out in the ordering of the *Homage*) is the latter. It is for this that he serves Pound as a persona, not in his capacity as love poet. The two themes are woven together to produce variety, but the choice of theme for the opening and the close of the sequence makes Pound's critical intention clear. It was not this strategy, however, but rather Pound's tactics of creative translation that shocked the conventional. The diction, the versification, even the "mistakes" were all so different from what readers of translations from Latin were used to that it is worthwhile considering each of these in some detail.

One well might begin with the diction, for it is difficult to overemphasize the revolutionary character of the language that Pound brought to the translation of Propertius. Latin poetry had suffered, and still suffers, from poeticizers, from dilute Miltonism, Swinburnism, and much Victorian verse practice in general. As a consequence, there hangs still a factitious mist, difficult to clear away, between our modern sensibility and the sensibility of the Roman poets. Much of the apparatus of Roman poetry has been absorbed into English literature and there undergone strange vicissitudes. This apparatus of mythological figures, forms of expression, stock epithets, etc., was taken over from English sources, mainly from Milton, by the mechanical verse translators of not many years ago, working as usual in a poetic diction a half century out of date, and it tends even now to inhibit any natural feeling or any perception of freshness which we might by hard work achieve for the original apparatus as found in Roman poets. Pound's diction served to remove from Propertius a sort of linguistic veil. After we have read the *Homage,* it is impossible for us to see Propertius in the same light. We cease to render down the "hard" poetry of the Latin into a soft romantic classicism. In this sense at least Pound's boast that the *Homage* has "scholastic value" is quite true: we are a step nearer the real qualities of Propertius because we have taken away from him some factitious qualities which Victorian classical translations had imposed. As it happens, he has achieved this not by any deep insight into Latin poetry or by any great knowledge of the Latin language but by feeling for poetry itself and the poetic language of his own tradition.

In *Personae,* Pound's collected shorter poems, there is an interesting early translation of Propertius (written between 1908 and 1910), which allows us to trace the development of Pound's diction in the translation of Latin poetry. It translates Propertius II, 28/47–56, which is retranslated in Section IX, 2, of the *Homage.*

In *Personae* (p. 52) it is headed:

Prayer for His Lady's Life
From Propertius, *Elegiae,* Lib. III, 26

Here let thy clemency, Persephone, hold firm,
Do thou, Pluto, bring here no greater harshness.
So many thousand beauties are gone down to Avernus,
Ye might let one remain above with us.

With you is Iope, with you the white-gleaming Tyro,
With you is Europa and the shameless Pasiphae,
And all the fair from Troy and all from Achaia,
From the sundered realms, of Thebes and of aged Priamus;
And all the maidens of Rome, as many as they were,
They died and the greed of your flame consumes them.

> *Here let thy clemency, Persephone, hold firm,*
> *Do thou, Pluto, bring here no greater harshness.*
> *So many thousand fair are gone down to Avernus,*
> *Ye might let one remain above with us.*

This becomes in the *Homage:*

> Persephone and Dis, Dis, have mercy upon her,
> There are enough women in hell,
>   quite enough beautiful women,
> Iope, and Tyro, and Pasiphae, and the formal girls of Achaia,
> And out of the Troad, and from the Campania,
> Death has his tooth in the lot,
>   Avernus lusts for the lot of them.
> Beauty is not eternal, no man has perennial fortune,
> Slow foot, or swift foot, death delays but for a season.
>
>   (Section IX, 2)

The second version is greatly preferable to the first, and for reasons easily explicable. The movement is surer, and the language more forthright, spare, unaffected, and modern in tone. It represents a movement away from the traditional translationese. Yet the first attempt is interesting in throwing light on some of the techniques Pound continued to make use of in the *Homage* itself. In particular, this very use of some translationese (e.g., *let thy clemency . . . hold firm* for *tua . . . maneat clementia,* and *as many as they were* for *quaecumque erat in numero*) is continued on a smaller scale to bring about certain effects in the *Homage.* The diction, which as used in prose-poetic translations by the Victorians was boring, dull, and lifeless, is used by Pound in a context of a modern idiom with great poetic effect. The result is to produce a poetic diction which conveys simultaneously a contemporary air (which was part of Pound's aim in bringing Propertius to life as a poet) and also an air of belonging to a different culture and civilization, relying in this upon some new controlled stock—responses to these elements of translationese. Because of this diction even the mythology, so unapproachable usually to the modern reader, seems both natural in its context and possessed for once of some poetic vitality.

Because Pound's style is an individual creation and emerges from a living language which is felt in all its nuances, and which has for background the colloquial speech of everyday, although much more ambitious, it offers several further and easily defined advantages over the artificial poetic styles exemplified in the previous translations of Propertius. For example, it represents adequately the considerable colloquial elements perceptible in Propertius' use of language. In this area at least Pound comes closer to real translation than do many of the more accepted verse translators. Naturally this is done, as in eighteenth-century imitations, by a process of analogy; colloquial elements are present in both the original and the translation, but not necessarily in the same places. The tone of the poem as a whole is Pound's concern, not the local similarities between the *Homage* and the Propertian elegies. This is not to argue that Pound has anticipated modern research into Propertius' language; one should avoid claiming for Pound any more extensive knowledge of Latin than he himself would claim. What may, however, be claimed for him is an intuitive flair for language and in particular the language of poetry; it is this which led him to the right language to express the sensibility he discerned in Propertius through the veils of a foreign, and in more significant ways *alien,* tongue. That this colloquial tone in Propertius is not immediately clear is due to the difficulties of a dead language. But that it is there and that Pound brings it out seems undeniable.

For evidence of Pound's ability to handle the more impassioned and "sonorous" areas of Propertius, one need only refer the reader to the poem itself. One further feature of Pound's diction, however, might be pointed out: this is its power to convey Pound's critical reading of Propertius when it discerns in the Roman poet what is normally unnoticed or neglected, the irony, wit, and mock-heroic tone. As Pound's language is in a way our own living language "charged with meaning to the utmost degree," he can utilize all the infinite range of effects which are possible only in a language with which one is perfectly familiar. These effects he can deploy to represent those elements in the

Roman poet which he intuitively perceives—and represent with a subtlety debarred to those working in an artificial idiom which is not, strictly speaking, their own. He knows the emotive connotations of the vocabulary inwardly, and can enforce the strictest control of their effect in the poetry and on the reader. The polysyllabic formality of phrases like *monumental effigies, elucidation, adornment, chicane, orfevrerie, escritoires,* etc., are counterpointed by the flatly colloquial ring of phrases like *I guzzle with out-stretched ears, my little mouth shall gobble, twiddles the spiked wheel, say nasty things,* and so on. The possible range of effects are many, but the most obvious is the ironic deflation of the grandiose gesture. Weaving in and out of these two obvious stylistic elements move the alien strands of translationese, which add distance to and damn, not the clichés of passion, as Kenner suggests, but the clichés of the poeticizers which Propertius as well as Pound had set his face against. It parodies the high-sounding diction of translators by setting it against the locutions and rhythms of contemporary speech, much as Eliot and Laforgue used the impressive Elizabethan and the sonorous romantic phrases to point a contrast or to tell a tale.

The effects are most obviously scored by the line lengths and the indentations which indicate the reading speed and tone. Punctuation, in particular the use of inverted commas, is relevant to this (n.b. Sections II and V, 1). These are, as it were, the lifted eyebrows that greet ironically the claim:

If I have not the faculty, "The bare attempt would be praiseworthy."

A similar but slighter example is the way Pound effects a local sophistication in the poem. Here the diction is characterized by certain modern terms, adjectives which in literary jargon have taken on the connotation Pound desires for reproducing an equivalent feeling which he finds in Propertius. This explains the anachronism which so vexed at least one classical scholar:

> Go on, to Ascraeus' prescription, the ancient, respected, Wordsworthian.

One unfortunate result, however, of the two versions of Section IX, 2 (quoted above) was an excessive critical attention to that area of the poem to the neglect of the whole. Much was said about the versification of the sequence which applies, if at all, simply to that particular section and which if applied to the whole is revealed as nonsense. In particular there is the assertion (made originally by Mr. Ronald Bottrall) that the *Homage* is "written in a subtle approximation to Latin elegiacs."[4] This notion was developed at length by Mr. A. Alvarez: "He is literally writing Latin verse in English, using the same quality of language that he finds in Propertius—colloquial, resonant, or ironic—and using it in what is basically a Latin metre . . ."[5] Alvarez points to

> There are quite enough women in hell,
>   quite enough beautiful women

and

> Death has his tooth in the lot,
>   Avernus lusts for the lot of them . . .

as examples of

more or less regular elegiac pentameters, less regular only because they have been accommodated to the cadence of the English idiom. So much has Pound made the Latin verse his own that the foreign quantitative metre emphasizes the native speaking emphasis: for example, in the first line the caesura is used to administer the ironic shock of the word "hell" . . .

Now in fact this use of the caesura can be seen in much of Pound's other verse where there is no question of an approximation to Latin elegiacs. Moreover, although the first halves of the two lines quoted have a resemblance to the first half of a Latin pentameter, with the rise or em-

---

[4] "XXX Cantos of Ezra Pound: An Incursion into Poetics," reprinted in *Determinations,* edited by F. R. Leavis (1934), pp. 179–198.

[5] *The Shaping Spirit* (London, 1958), pp. 53–55.

phasis on the last syllable there, yet the second halves of those lines
have that second expected final rise so blurred by further syllables
that we have a tailing off, a dying fall, which is the more effective
because of that "shock" at the caesura. This is not the effect of a regular
pentameter. In any case a foreign quantitative metre is not carried
across to emphasize the native speaking emphasis (except in certain
artificial experiments). Pound would have been mistaken had he tried
any "subtle approximation to Latin elegiacs." In any case he did no
such thing, as a glance at the last two lines of that section of the
Homage makes clear.

> Beauty is not eternal, no man has perennial fortune
> Slow foot, or swift foot, death delays but for a season.

If further proof were needed, a reading of Section VII of the *Homage*
would provide it, where the speed and changes of tempo are quite
different from anything the elegiac couplet is capable of. The verse
patterns of the *Homage* are far more varied than they could be if the
above assertions were true; compare, for example, the weighty and
solemn rhythms of Section II with the light, quick tempo of Section X.
The form of the *Homage* is vers libre of a certain sort, and it amply
illustrates Eliot's comment that no *vers* is *libre* for the man who wants
to do a good job.

A more profitable way of looking at the vers libre that Pound adopts
as a substitute for the elegiac couplets of his original is to consider it in
terms of sense units. The Latin elegiac couplet tends to be complete in
sense, and complete in grammar. Each two-line unit is a closed system,
and even this system often falls into two units, the second line frequently
illustrating or summarizing the first. It can and does lead to pleonasm
and padding (most notably in Ovid), vices which Pound is often
concerned to eliminate. This militates against making a proper generalization about Pound's verse tactics and his treatment of what he is
translating. But where such vices are not in question and where Pound

is not using certain other techniques for particular purposes, we find a tendency toward a long line followed by a shorter line (occasionally two shorter lines); this is not dictated by the Latin verse pattern but by the *sense pattern*. The various poetic effects of the Latin couplet, where it is not simply repeating or illustrating the thought of the hexameter in the pentameter, tend to come in the pentameter and in particular in the last half of that line. An example or two will show this (I confine myself to the parts of Propertius translated by Pound):

> Andromede monstris fuerat devota marinis:
> haec eadem Persei *nobilis uxor erat*

Which becomes in Section VIII:

> Andromeda was offered to a sea-serpent
> and *respectably* married to Perseus.

Again,

> quod si forte tibi properarint fata quietem
> illa sepulturae fata beata tuae

becomes

> What if your fates are accelerated;
> your quiet hour put forward,
> You may find interment pleasing ...

(the first two lines as the indentation indicates are the equivalent of the longer line). Pound's lines thus become not a subtle approximation to Latin elegiacs considered as meter but a more or less accurate matching in English of the sense pattern.

Even where it is simply a question of reiteration of the basic thought of the hexameter in the pentameter, Pound follows the thought pattern in his verse.

Thus in Section VIII:

> Num sibi collatam doluit Venus ipsa paremque?
> per se formosis invidiosa dea est

becomes

> Was Venus exacerbated by the existence of a comparable equal?
> Is the ornamental goddess full of envy?

This last line is not an approximation to a pentameter by any criterion. So although there occur occasionally lines which can be read as English equivalents of pentameter lines or even half-hexameter lines, it is not true that Pound throughout the *Homage* is deliberately producing an approximation to the Latin elegiac couplet in English. He is following the sense pattern which the elegiac couplet produces, and not always this, if the sense is repetitive or padded, or if he wishes to secure larger effects which are incompatible with this general tendency.

The poetic practice of Pound, and of many similar poets of the first half of the twentieth century, is based to a large extent upon two principles. The first is the principle of the image and the second is the principle that Yvor Winters has called "associative structure."

A great deal has been written on the first, not only by the founders of the Imagist movement (with their slogans such as that of Wyndam Lewis—*The Image is the primary pigment of poetry*) but also by recent critics. But the elaborate theories constructed by the Imagist movement are not relevant to our present purpose: for it is not a question of getting clear the aims of Imagism, but rather of seeing how the Imagists' work isolated a certain technique. And Pound's reports of his reading and critical perceptions at the time should discourage one from an over-elaborate investigation of the philosophical influences on the movement (cf., e.g., *Make It New*, p. 361). Historical explanations and critical expositions even by Pound himself are not germane to our limited purposes. *Never trust the artist, trust the tale* is a commendable attitude to theories of writing poetry and explaining how poetry came to be written. Success is the only justification and a technique is justified if it is successful.

All that need be said is that the Imagists were taking what has always been an important part of poetry, and concentrating and refining it for their own poetic purposes, which were, historically, to get away from certain poetic modes prevalent at that time. They wished to renew the sensuousness and concreteness of poetry of which a most valuable part to them lay in clear, precise imagery. In devoting themselves so wholeheartedly to what they saw as an older tradition opposed to sloppy and muddled romanticism, they were encouraged by the example of Chinese and Japanese poetry.

Two of Pound's slogans may be offered as illustration:

1. Direct treatment of the "thing" whether subjective or objective.
2. To use absolutely no word that does not contribute to the presentation.

Poetry, Aristotle noted, offers us universals, although it works through apparently individual things, giving the universal, as it were, a local habitation and a name (*Poetics* 1451 ab): Othello *is* jealousy. Similarly the image, for Pound, should embody a precise particular, but it is for general, i.e., poetic, purposes. Usually with the Imagists it was to embody a certain emotion or a certain state of mind by means of a precise picture. The image was, to use a term of Eliot's, the "objective correlative" which is or becomes the formula of a particular emotion.

Because of the irrelevant historical connotations of the term Imagism, Pound took to using the term *phanopoeia* for this poetic element. This with *melopoeia* and *logopoeia* covered the whole range of poetry. Whatever the deficiencies of the analysis for the critic, it was useful for the poetic technician, and certain experiments indicate its usefulness. Three poems written under its aegis are to be found in *Personae* (1952, pp. 179–180): they are not impressive, but provide interesting illustrations of what becomes an important technique in the *Homage*.

This concern for exact presentation, the hatred of imprecision and superfluous rhetoric, does very well as a slogan and indeed had its good practical results. This is not, however, to say that there is in Pound nothing otiose or blurred. The *Homage,* for example, has its poetic inaccuracies, its areas of meaninglessness *("much conversation is as good as having a home"),* which fly in the face of this program. The difficulty arises when we believe in a poet's program and try anything but honesty to make his general performance square with his best work and his theories. When I say then that Pound's "imagism" leads to a clearer, more poetic use of Propertius' imagery, I refer to the best areas of the poem. I am not ignoring the blemishes of the work, but pointing out the aim and explaining the considerable achievement—*every beginning is a different kind of failure.*

Here is one example of how the image is used in the *Homage.* In Section III Propertius is summoned at midnight to his mistress at Tibur—in the original the verse continues *"where the gleaming summits display their double towers, and the water of Anio tumbles into spacious pools."* This is simply legitimate ornament, not descriptive definition, even though a logical connection is attempted by the word *where.* It is in fact an image which occurs to Propertius at the thought of Tibur. Its status as an image is therefore brought out by Pound as follows:

> Midnight, and a letter comes to me from our mistress:
> Telling me to come to Tibur:
> > *At* once!!
> "Bright tips reach up from twin towers,
> Anienan spring water falls into flat-spread pools."

Once we are used to this technique, it becomes perfectly comprehensible and is as effective as the more traditional way of working the image, grammatically as it were, into the poem, and producing a seemingly necessary connection.

This example leads on to the second principle. What has happened is that what Pound calls the "rhetorical" connection has been abolished. The image is the important thing, the connective is no more than a grammatical justification to beguile the reader into accepting it as following logically on the mention of Tibur. And this, to Pound, is a prose technique. Pound has described poetry as "language charged with meaning to the utmost degree": this entails the abolition of the poetically unnecessary. A poem is not an argument; even genuine as well as factitious connections may be abolished in favor of more "poetic" links—in this case, juxtaposition. The emotional effect or the precise picture is still there, but the link is now intuitively, not discursively, grasped.

The second principle may thus be seen as the principle on which the image (as in the above example) is introduced into the poem, but its application extends much further. Winters, as I remarked earlier, has called it the principle of "Associative Structure" and referred it to the empiricist notion that all our ideas arise from the constant association of sense impressions. Not only is this explanation unlikely, however, as an explanation of the facts of literary history, but if taken seriously as a way of seeing the phenomenon it is liable to mislead. It is true that in Hume, for example, the constant association of certain events replaces the notion of a necessary relation between cause and effect. But for Hume this is a brute fact of nature, and thus far inexplicable. To suggest, as Winters might on this analogy, that the principle used in modern poetry to associate apparently disconnected ideas implies an absence of necessary relation or (as might be implied by his choice of words) some purely psychological and therefore poetically random association is surely wrong. There are relations in fact, and Pound's emphasis on craftsmanship as opposed to unconscious poetic inspiration underlines this. Where Winters' suggestion is valuable is in the contrast he draws between the modern method and the rational structure of Classical and Renaissance writing. This difference can be pin-pointed in the example quoted above. The connective *where* produces an illusion of necessary and logical sequence of ideas, but it is the image which is important, not the connective. In the *Homage* the link ceases to be a grammatical link and becomes instead a purely emotional or pictorial link. It is on the necessity of this link that its success is still to be judged, but even in the more traditional technique (with the grammatical link supplied) the same judgment has to be made about the appropriateness of the image or new theme. The poetic logic is still important, even though at first modern poetry seems much more abrupt and inconsequential when compared to the steady determined "logical" development of, say, eighteenth-century poems. But that the general idea of simple juxtaposition of themes and images is a recognized poetic method may be seen by looking at certain classical poems (e.g., Horace, *Odes* I, 4), which despite certain formal connective devices are essentially this.

The sort of poetry we find in the *Homage* makes violent use of emotional linkage. All formal and grammatical connection may vanish in the interests of the harder poetical impact. But the juxtaposition of apparently unrelated subjects can be a significant juxtaposition with its own logic. The new theme affects the preceding theme and modifies the feeling of the whole poem. As we have seen, the idea is not novel and is, indeed, appropriate to a translation of Propertius, a poet whose abrupt transitions inside an elergy are very noticeable, even though within the couplet the more rhetorical form prevails. It is in effect an alternative to the more discursive development which explains itself, although this "explanation" is sometimes apparent more than real—for why this theme is grammatically linked to that may be just as much a critical problem as the more abrupt juxtaposition.

With these two principles in mind any particular difficult section of the *Homage* becomes clearer. Such a section may be seen as imitating in small the unity of the whole sequence, which, as we have said, depends for its meaning on a juxtaposition of private and public themes in a significant pattern. And the very sequence conveys its poetic meaning. Patently a prose or verse introduction could be added to each section which might make it all clearer, but this is not the poet's function. Poems are not paraphrasable in this way, and the omission of the grammatical framework is, as it were, a rejection of the rhetorical and the nonpoetic, whether prose or verse.

Section XI illustrates best these principles, as well as the techniques of compression and omission, examined earlier. The parts of Propertius on which it is based may be tabulated briefly: I. 15, II. 30, II. 32, II. 30, II. 32, and II. 24. *Elegy* I. 15 is a long complaint: "'I have often feared many things hard to bear from your fickleness (*levitas*), Cynthia, but never yet this perfidy'." Propertius then contrasts Cynthia's behavior with the better behavior of certain mythological heroines. Her pretenses of innocence are useless. He, however, will never change, and he concludes: "'It is by those eyes I am perishing, a warning to lovers like me that safety lies, alas, in believing no blandishments'."

Pound omits completely the mythological arguments and preserves only the bare bones of the situation, heightening Propertius' warning by a vivid image which is only half explicit in Propertius:

> The harsh acts of your levity!
> Many and many.
> I am hung here, a scarecrow for lovers.

This constitutes the whole of Part 1 of the Section, the most extreme example of compression in the whole poem.

Part 2 translates the first eight lines of II. 30, which are (literally):

Where are you flying to, in your madness? Flight is impossible: you may fly to Tanais, yet Love will ever follow you. Riding in air on the back of Pegasus will not avail; not though your feet be furnished with wings like Perseus, not though the breezes, cleft by your winged heels, waft you with a lofty flight like Mercury's, will it be of use. Love is always hovering over your head: he hovers over a lover, and alights with all his weight on free necks.

This becomes:

> Escape! There is, O Idiot, no escape,
> Flee if you like into Ranaus—desire will follow you thither,

> Though you heave into the air upon the gilded Pegasean back,
> Though you had the feathery sandals of Perseus
> To lift you up through split air.
> The high tracks of Hermes would not afford you shelter.
> Amor stands upon you, Love drives upon lovers,
>   a heavy mass on free necks.

Instead of continuing with II. 30, which goes on to describe the complaisance of Love when approached in the right spirit and to defend love and all that goes with it as a way of life, Pound cuts to line 17 of II. 32, in which Cynthia is trying to escape not Love itself but her jealous lover. This reinforces the earlier theme. Literally it runs: "It is not from the city you are so madly eager to escape, but from my sight. Your efforts are useless: the snares you are laying for me are in vain: you are idly spreading nets for me that I am well aware of—I am experienced." This becomes:

> It is our eyes you flee, not the city,
> You do nothing, you plot inane schemes against me,
> Languidly you stretch out the snare
>   with which I am already familiar, . . .

This elegy had begun with Cynthia's journeys from the city on some religious pretext; Propertius is jealous. He then proceeds to rationalise this jealousy into a concern for her good name (the typical desire to keep the beloved on the straight and narrow path). He continues, therefore:

It is not, however, for myself that I care; it is that you will suffer a loss of your good name in proportion to your deserts. A report of you that lately came to my ears grieved me: in the whole city there was not a good word about you. But (you will say) you should not believe hostile tongues; beautiful women have always had to pay the penalty of scandal.

All this is vividly compressed and becomes:

> Rumours of you throughout the city,
>   and no good rumour among them.

"You should not believe hostile tongues."
"Beauty is slander's cock-shy."
"All lovely women have known this . . ."

Pound indicates by the punctuation that he takes it that Cynthia was speaking. Propertius then apparently accepts this beautiful piece of feminine illogicality and begins to defend Cynthia's conduct and possible peccadilloes by imagining far worse crimes she has *not* committed and adducing mythological examples of high fornication. Literally: "Your character has not been damned by poison being found upon you: Phoebus, you will bear witness that you see [her with] untainted hands. And if one or two nights have been spent in long lovemaking, I am not one to be moved by slight offences."

The poison motif Pound misunderstands or transposes to apply to the venomous tongues already spoken of and to defend Cynthia's innocence in all important respects. The point about her minor infidelities is probably misunderstood by Pound; it is taken as meaning that a night of love would cause Propertius to forgive her offenses; in any case it is transferred to the very end of the section.

Thus Pound:

"Your glory is not outblotted by venom,"
"Phoebus our witness, your hands are unspotted."

Propertius' defense of Cynthia is conducted largely on the mythological level; in the *Homage* it is compressed into two examples: "The daughter of Tyndarus left her home for a foreign lover, yet she was brought back alive and uncondemned. Venus herself is said to have been seduced by Mars' lust, yet she remained an honest woman in heaven as before . . . —"

A foreign lover brought down Helen's kingdom
and she was led back living home;
The Cytharean brought low by Mars' lechery
reigns in respectable heavens, . . .

Pound returns to II. 30 for his material; there Propertius was left defending love as a way of life. But he abruptly complains that Cynthia is preparing to leave him: "Are you preparing to move through Phrygian waves, you hard heart, to seek the Eastern shores of the Hyrcanian Sea?" These lines are almost certainly out of place here; in any case, Pound only uses them much later to take up the theme of escape from Love. Propertius presumably went straight on to ask why he should be ashamed of being content with one mistress—Love is to blame, not he—and to picture Cynthia and himself living contentedly on Mount Helicon. "Ah, Cynthia, if only you would choose to dwell with me in dewy caverns on a mossy hill: there you shall see the tuneful sisters cling to the rocks and sing of the sweet clandestine loves of ancient Jove: of how he was consumed with love for Semele, how madly fond of Io and how, in the form of a bird, he flew to the halls of Troy . . . " These exploits too are a defense for Propertius. And the Muses (or at least Calliope) are no strangers to love.

All this is compressed: only the bare images are used to sketch an attempt to get away from the evil tongues and the necessity of defending Cynthia against them. The similarity of theme of the two elegies allow the pastiche to work very well.

> Oh, oh, and enough of this,
> by dew-spread caverns,
> The Muses clinging to the mossy ridges;
> to the ledge of the rocks;

And still harping on the theme of the inescapability of love Pound allows the mythological examples of II. 30 to express this in a series of finely pared images:

> Zeus' clever rapes, in the old days,
> combusted Semeles, of Io strayed.
> Of how the bird flew from Trojan rafters.

And there is even a return to the examples of divine fornication in II. 32 for another image, the Latin grossly distorted. Propertius there

continued: "Although Mount Ida can say a goddess loved the shepherd
Paris and lay with him among the flocks of his fold" (referring to
Oenone, although Mueller punctuates as though it were Venus). Pound
(rather humorously) takes it as

> Ida has lain with a shepherd, she has slept among sheep . . .

Despite the mistake over the name, the picture is identical in significance.

Finally, to take up the original theme of the inescapability of love,
Pound uses the misplaced scrap mentioned earlier, which becomes:

> Even there, no escape
> Not the Hyrcanian seaboard, not in seeking
> the shore of Eos

And follows this with the misunderstood complaisant remark of
Propertius:

> All things are forgiven for one night of your games . . .

And hunting for a further image, he constructs one from four lines in
II. 24 which describe Cynthia's rapacity:

> Though you walk in the Via Sacra, with a peacock's tail for a fan.

Pound means here to suggest that Cynthia's polygamous inclinations
may be carried to the extent of openly prostituting herself (the Sacra Via
was a well-known haunt of whores. Cf., Prop. II. 23. 15-16).

This last example is typical of the method. Propertius is plundered for
striking images which are then used to add to an original Propertian
theme some new element. This whole section is concerned with the
ineluctable power of Love. The two original Propertian elegies were on
a similar theme. II. 30 suggested that Love was inescapable, that he
offered a way of life, that even deities knew his power and that a
mistress was a source of inspiration. II. 32 was a demonstration of
jealousy, then of concern and forgiveness for infidelity, and this

forgiveness was justified by mythical and historical examples of immoral behaviour—how could Cynthia be expected to behave any better? In XI. 1 there is just the stark image of the helpless victim of Love. In XI. 2 a series of images stress the point: there is no escape from Love. Then the lover replaces love—the beloved cannot escape him and yet, as he is so much in love, her attempts to betray him are forgiven. And rightly, for Love holds dominion over heroine and goddess. There is then an attempt to leave behind the evil tongues, to accept love for what it is in some idyllic spot where the Muses are. For love is always with us, even Jove felt its power, and its power could produce tragedy—"combusted Semeles, Io strayed"—as well as indignity—"Ida has lain with a shepherd." Thus there is no escape. But as the poet is in love, all may be forgiven, even the grossest betrayals for the least-considered favors.

The images are bare and concise, but they are all at the service of the one important idea:

> Escape! There is, O Idiot, no escape . . .

Finally, one comes to the most shocking of all Pound's tactics of translation—his errors. Actually, the attention paid to this feature of the *Homage* has been ridiculous. Pound pointed out that he was not doing a crib or trot of the poems; he was not a translator in the sense that one of his most important duties was fidelity to the original. This fidelity, be it said, is normally interpreted in a narrow sense—provided that the denotation of a translation corresponds with the denotation of the original, a translation will be accepted as accurate even though the emotional color, poetic language, and so on are completely alien to the original. Pedestrian prose becomes an acceptable vehicle for Homer, Swinburnian word music the basis of an accepted and praised version of Euripides. On this score Pound is arguably more "accurate" than many translators. At least he offers poetry for poetry.

There are several ways of reducing the apparently large number of misrenderings which strike the eye of the classical reader when he compares the *Homage* with his text of Propertius. The text used by Pound was the 1892 Teubner text of Lucian Mueller, a text substantially different from most modern texts, not only in the readings and the line transpositions which it adopts, but also in its division and numbering of the elegies. Once this is appreciated, the *Homage* becomes rather less of a patchwork than modern critics have believed. Where Pound begins or ends a section is often to be explained by a suggested lacuna in Mueller or Mueller's transposition of our opening lines to the close of the preceding elegy. Section VI, e.g., apparently omits the first sixteen lines of Propertius II. 13, but it begins where Mueller begins a new elegy (III. 5 in his enumeration, following Lachmann). Some seeming amalgamations of two elegies by Pound, e.g., of III. 1 and 2, may be similarly defended; these were printed by Mueller as IV. 1. Mueller may be faulted by modern textual editors, but this cannot be a criticism of Pound. His was a respectable text—*quot editores tot Propertii.*

There are also some unexpected translations which can be defended on good philological grounds.[6]

In Section I, *gaudeat ut solito tacta puella sono* (may my mistress, touched, rejoice in the familiar music) is translated by Pound in such a way that *tacta puella* becomes "the devirginated young ladies." The plural is easily explained by Pound's tendency to distil from what is for Propertius a private and particular situation a more general view. But in *tacta* there is a deliberate ambiguity: it means, rather pleonastically, "touched" (by the familiar music) and simultaneously suggests the opposite of *virgo intacta* (a classical phrase, cf. Catullus, 62, 45); thus *tactus* has a sexual meaning, frequently found in classical Latin. This perception of such ambiguities was perhaps one of the reasons for

---

[6] An excellent discussion of the various mistakes is to be found in Mr. L. J. Richardson's article in the *Yale Poetry Review* 6 (1947), pp. 22 ff. Despite my disagreements with his conception of the significance of the "mistakes," Richardson throws considerable light on how they occur.

Pound's attribution to Propertius of *logopoeia*, but for the moment the
general question may be forgotten in order to concentrate on Pound's
tactics for translating such ambiguities. Patently one of the two meanings must go, and Pound rightly prefers to sacrifice the more pleonastic
for the more suggestive. The actual wit he expresses by the choice of a
phrase which relies on certain social connotations brought into juxtaposition; it does not require the text to appreciate it. But the translation
itself cannot be called a mistake because the meaning he has used is
arguably there in the context.

But even so there are still a large number of places where Pound does
not reproduce the actual or even the suggested meaning of the Latin.
Sometimes this is important and sometimes not. Unimportant instances
(most of which are obvious if one compares the text and a literal
translation) are the misspellings of classical proper names, the mis-
readings of nonfunctional tenses and the confusing of mythological and
historical references. These neither obscure the logic of a section nor
affect its poetic impact. They are misleading only if the *Homage* is used
as a crib, which it never will be. It must be admitted of course that this
sort of thing springs partly from a deliberate and obstinate defiance of
scholarly standards; unlike Joyce, Pound is resolutely antiacademic—
"the letter killeth"—and there are more personal reasons we need not
go into. Hence he persists in such gestures as *Bloughram* for *Blougram*
in *Mauberley* and *Polydmantus* for the more correct form *Polydamas*
printed in Section I on its first appearance.[7] Pound's principles,
however, put some of these errors in their proper perspective. Mythology
is not an exact science nor is it a Holy Writ with authorized versions;
this is some justification of his inexact use of mythology. Even in
classical poets it is often used simply for ornament or the production of a

[7] In a recent letter to me Pound has defended some such defiances of the
original forms on the grounds that his forms give in English a "better sound" and
that sometimes the retention of the original meaning exactly (e.g., Section
I—*Oetian gods* for Propertius' *Oetian God*, i.e., Hercules) "wd . . . bitch the
movement of the verse."

certain romantic effect. Obscure references and names, whether accurate or inaccurate, still reverberate only as a confused and impressive set of associations, dimly apprehended. Pound's carefree impressionism touches our sensibilities adequately enough, for few of us are trained in an exact knowledge of obscure mythology.

In general it may be said that considering the frequency of these minor inaccuracies it is surprising how much Pound appreciates in each case what the line is to imply and contribute to the poetic strategy of the whole. Sometimes indeed a mistake will sharpen a piece of irony or deflate some cliché or some piece of conventional Augustan deference on the part of Propertius. It is difficult then to decide how unconscious or careless or deliberate the misrendering is. There are, however, some (rare) instances where the mistake does interfere with the poetic logic, making it more difficult to connect one thought with another. Propertius is obscure in his transitions, Pound even more and deliberately so, and these misrenderings can hinder the reader's grasp of the poem's development where a more correct representation of Propertius' meaning would not, and this, in my opinion, without detriment to the tone or poetry. A glance at Propertius' text will often clear up instantly some puzzling local difficulty and still leave one with the impression that the poem is not improved at this point by the obscurity even though it yields to patient scrutiny. Pound's impatient freshness and eagerness do have some disadvantages; both the correct and the incorrect translation would make the same contribution to the whole section, but Pound has made no concessions to sticklers for accuracy.

Such things might happen in any verse translation; there is, however, a really important and interesting category of "mistakes"—the apparent "howlers"—which have irritated the pedantic beyond measure. Those with enough sense of humor to see that they cannot be unconscious mistranslations regard this as the perverse side of the *Homage;* those with less regard them as the most crass examples of the many mistakes which may be catalogued.

Certain apparent pieces of bad construing may be due not to an ignorance of syntax and concord, but to an attention to the Latin word order in the interests of Pound's notion of *melopoeia*. *Coan ghosts of Philetas,* e.g., in Section I, reproduces more clearly the ordering of *Coi sacra Philetae.* In fact the line succeeds rhythmically and the meaning is not changed.

There seems implicit in certain of Pound's practices a theory that homophones in a language (e.g., *canes*—"you will sing" and *canes*— "dogs") somehow infect each other and thus each meaning carries the contagion of the other. Now there can be a deliberate use of homophones in particular contexts to produce the sort of poetic ambiguity Empson has analyzed (and which may be found, of course in Propertius, as in most poets). Verbal wit employs the same linguistic phenomenon and the unconscious can utilize it for its own purposes in the psycho-pathology of everyday life. Occasionally too an obscene word will infect its harmless homophone, but in general such automatic infection does not happen; normally the possible ambiguity of homophones has to be purposely utilized in a complex unit of sound and meaning for this to happen—words only mean in a sentence and the context dictates and limits the ranges of meaning of the word. Except in the cases outlined above we do not have to brush away the other meanings to get at the intended meaning, particularly in a language with which one is famil-iar. Now this has relevance to bilingual contexts and to the explanations given of certain of Pound's mistranslations.

One sort of mistranslation which seems to work on this principle, if we assume it is not a simple mistake, is in Section II. There Pound translates *nocturnaeque canes ebria signa fugae* (you will sing of the drunken evidence of a nocturnal escapade) by "Night dogs, the marks of a drunken scurry." But by no stretch of the imagination could Propertius have worked for this connotation; the Latin simply does not admit of any ambiguity here, as was perhaps intended in the *tacta puella* of Section I. The theory of homophones cannot support it. What does justify it in the context is success, the greater vividness of the image.

A similar sort of mistranslation involves the use of similarities in the Latin to certain English words. For example, in Section II, Pound translates *ora Philetaea nostra rigavit aqua* by "Stiffened our face with the backwash of Philetas the Coan." *Rigavit* means simply "to mois-ten." Pound relies here on the connotation of "rigid" in English and intensifies the simple meaning of the Latin to give the line an overtone of the stiffening of a poetic resolve. There is, in fact, no need to postulate a theory for these changes or bad philology; Pound simply uses a stray suggestion which crosses his mind—the provenance of it is unimportant —to intensify a poetic image and in particular to add something of his own feeling about the whole sequence to it.

This discounting of possible theories and the insistence that the justification of such misrenderings lies in their success is important for the last and most notable sets of mistranslations. First there is the collage of sense, which consists in taking a few of the Latin words, ignoring their grammatical connections and offering for the original meaning an impressionistic sentence which fits plausibly to what has gone before. Richardson quotes an example of this in Section I: for

> multi, Roma, tuas laudes annalibus addent,
> qui finem imperii Bacta futura canent

Pound has

> Annalists will continue to record Roman reputations,
> Celebrities from the Trans-Caucasus will belaud Roman celebrities, . . .

the second line of which is achieved by taking *Roma, laudes, imperii, Bactra,* ignoring their actual meaning in the context and producing a plausible and amusing line. The words serve simply to suggest an image. The technique is not unlike that of Apollinaire; any stray piece of knowledge or random image might serve to produce a line. Apollinaire's connection with the Cubists, his appreciation of an object as an assemblage of aspects, makes his technique reminiscent of the method of collage used by Picasso and Braque. Richardson's term "collage" for this technique of Pound's takes us back to the period at which the *Homage* was written. It also explains the additions which Pound makes to various lines, e.g., in Section I—for *Taenariis* . . . *columnis,* Pound gives us: "Taenarian columns from Laconia (associated with Neptune and Cerberus)." And the use of such marginalia is justified, if at all, by their success, and not because they explain anything or because, in the case of "the frigidaire patent" Pound added to later editions, they are a piece of irreverent nose-thumbing at myopic scholars.[8]

Once this is accepted, and the justification of the collage is seen in the ability of these lines to express more clearly Pound's concerns, which are an ironic extension and a deepening of the Propertian attitude, we may turn to more extreme examples of misrenderings which have a slightly different rationale.

In Section XII,

> tale facis carmen docta testudine quale
> Cynthius impositis temperat articulis

(literally: you produce such a poem as the Cynthian god plays, with his fingers on his artistic lyre) becomes in Pound

> Like a trained and performing tortoise,
> I would make verse in your fashion, if she should command it.

Richardson compares this sort of thing to the sophomore's technique of dealing with an unprepared passage; Kenner compares it to schoolboys' howlers. To the unscholarly reader English associations, incorrect but possible meanings of the Latin words, may come unbidden before he perceives the right and only meaning of what is on the page before him. These false scents, under the pressure of necessity in a class or even for amusement, may be used to produce a meaning which makes sense of a peculiar sort. It is indeed this possibility, the ingenuity

[8] A piece of information kindly communicated to me by Mr. Hugh Kenner.

of the young mind, and the almost ineradicable belief that the Romans and Greeks were strange people and one must not be surprised at anything they appear to say that are responsible for the numerous errors which can be made by schoolboys in translating Latin.

In the example just given the suggestions in the Latin which have allowed Pound to reach his result are roughly as follows: *docta/* "learned," and thus "trained"; *testudine/*"the tortoise-shell lyre," thus "tortoise"; *impositis articulis/*"the imposed articulation"; *Cynthius/* "Cynthian," thus "Cynthia"; *temperat/*"modulate," thus "tone down," "reduce my verse to your level."

Now such associations are possible, and can be evoked at will for purposes of amusement; it can become a sort of bilingual pun, and Kenner is right to point out the resemblance to the bilingual parony-masia of Joyce, although I do not think that this is a necessary or sufficient reason for Pound's employment of the technique. His sugges-tion, however, that "such vestigial surrealisms can never be cleaned out of our consciousness of a Latin poem" (except by complete familiarity with the text) is surely wrong. Such associations only arise, even with schoolboys, when there is, for instance, some striking resemblance between an English and a Latin word, or when the sense so far gleaned requires a wrong meaning from the Latin word to complete itself. But even if it were so always, and granted that this were the sort of suggestion Pound has used to construct his lines, it seems an arbitrary technique. Unless one can offer an explanation, and I do not think Pound's intentions were those of Joyce, a charge of perversity might lie.

Richardson's justification seems to be that there is some pleasure one may get from one's own mental convolutions when reading Latin, and that one's mistaken first ideas of a passage are of some value, and he concludes: "At the end, I confess, I must have the Latin before me if I am to get the most out of Pound" (*op. cit.* pp. 24–25). The first suggestion seems hardly relevant to poetry and the second has the disadvantage that the *Homage* ceases to be an independent work; it becomes a function of two texts juxtaposed. But the sequence is in general a poem in its own right; all we should require for its appreciation is what is there and the knowledge we bring to it for its understanding as a poem. We assume, with Aristotle, that the best kind of poetry is that which is most complete and self-sufficient. This applies equally to the great translations; if the original has to be read alongside the new poem, half the point of translation is lost. Any poet is entitled to assume an ideal reader, and that ideal reader would have all that was required to understand the work fully. There are *no* ideal readers, and although a knowledge of Propertius will deepen our understanding in many ways of the *Homage,* much as Eliot's notes help to some extent with *The Waste Land,* yet however difficult a poem, it is a public poem, not an esoteric private poem. To require the text always at hand to appreciate it would make it the latter.

Kenner seems to hint at an explanation in the *logopoeia* that Pound finds in Propertius, an "elaborate contextual wit." [9] But although there is a case for this and Pound's reproduction of it in the *Homage,* such irrational puns can only reproduce *logopoeia* if we have the adventitious aid of a text before us to see the play on words, and his explanation thus suffers from the same critical difficulty as Richardson's defense. In any case we cannot look to such local distortions of the Latin for the *logopoeia:* Pound himself specifically says: *"Logopoeia* does not translate; though the attitude of mind it expresses may pass through a paraphrase. Or one might say, you cannot translate it 'locally,' but having determined the original author's state of mind, you may or may not be able to find a derivative or an equivalent." Pound's equivalent is not this bilingual and irrational pun.

The justification of these passages is that here Pound is concerned to express more of himself, his feelings, his irony and bitterness. The method is purely heuristic, a way of allowing himself a leap into his own

[9] *The Poetry of Ezra Pound* (London, Faber & Faber, 1951), p. 149.

poetic concerns to the neglect of Propertius, while retaining a tiny thread of linguistic association with the original. The example quoted above is typical. Propertius throws out a deferential compliment to Virgil; although he does not wish to imitate his epic endeavors, he wants to use even him and similar poets as a justification of his own love poetry—they too have indulged in it. But Pound's dislike of Virgil, all he stands for, and those like him that Pound knew in his own time, is far more angry than Propertius' wry defensiveness. Defense is replaced by attack in the bitter irony of the "trained and performing tortoise," the savage glance at the *infamy* of such writing—"one must have resonance, resonance and sonority ... like a goose." Similar intrusions of the harder attitude of Pound may be seen in Section II. Propertius' *hiscere* ("tell of," for only chasms "yawn" with this word in Latin) suffers a sea-change to express Pound's distaste for epic Roman subjects:

> Alba, your kings and the realms your folk
>   have constructed with such industry
> Shall be *yawned* out on my lyre
>   with such industry.

Such examples then are not an ironic reflection of "the ghosts that dance before schoolboys' eyes" nor an exploration of zones of consciousness, but the utilization of a simple technique for Pound's poetic purposes and personal concerns: there is no need to understand or even see the bilingual pun, although we may derive some nonpoetic pleasure from so doing. Insofar as they produce poetry and express what Pound wants to express, they are justified—and some of the most striking lines occur in these areas. This is how Pound works; it allows him less restraint when he wishes to depart from Propertius; it provides useful suggestions for his lines; but it is not a deliberate exercise in wit for the classically trained. Pound does use a form of pun elsewhere and the example is illuminating; in *Mauberley:*

> τίν ἄνδρα τίν᾽ ἥſωα τίνα θεόν
> What god, man, or hero
> Shall I place a tin wreath upon!

is a bilingual pun, but it is not expertise. The tin wreath is as damning as a paper crown, but it is suggested by the adapted Pindaric line from the second Olympian, and the pun on the two contrasting implications reinforces the irony and contempt.

AMPHITRYON 38: SOME NOTES ON JEAN GIRAUDOUX AND MYTH

By Melvin J. Friedman

GILBERT HIGHET in *The Classical Tradition* points to two separate tendencies in modern myth-making. One he connects with the Symbolist poets and their inheritors (including Joyce and Eliot) who rely heavily on oblique parallels; the other he connects with the straightforward "reinterpreters" who redo classical myths in twentieth-century terms—occasionally in modern dress—most often as plays. The first is peculiarly contemporary, quite without literary ancestry. The second is merely a renewal of the urge to find inspiration and thematic direction from the classics. The difference, in short, is that the Symbolists are using myth to create a new form while the more traditional group is concerned only with the subject matter of the Greek legends.

T. S. Eliot has added "mythical method" to our critical vocabulary to express the first tendency. In his 1923 review of Joyce's *Ulysses* ("*Ulysses,* Order and Myth") he explains this new conception: "In using the myth in manipulating a continuous parallel between contemporaneity and antiquity, Mr. Joyce is pursuing a method which others must pursue after him. . . . Instead of narrative method, we may now use the mythical method." Eliot was thinking not only of Joyce here but probably of his own *Waste Land* and its French Symbolist progenitors. *The Odyssey* "continuous parallel" in *Ulysses* was obvious even to Joyce's earliest commentators like Valery Larbaud. Eliot's "program notes" following his poem made the classical allusions in *The Waste Land* readily accessible even to those who were unable to translate the Greek and Latin quotations found in the epigraph and elsewhere. Pound's *Cantos* follows Eliot's method with a vengeance, expanding a technique used in 434 lines to a lifetime of poetic research and technical improvisation. One can add *Finnegans Wake* to this list of works which thrives on oblique parallels.

This free use of "mythical method" in Joyce, Eliot, and Pound has offered literary critics the invitation to look for it elsewhere in modern literature. Carlos Baker finds a loose *Odyssey* parallel in Hemingway's *The Sun Also Rises*. Carvel Collins finds a convincing "inverse" application of material from Frazer's *The Golden Bough* in Faulkner's *As I Lay Dying*. In each case Greek myth enlarges the framework and even the texture of the novel. Some of our most responsible critics have re-evaluated literature in terms of myth; Northrop Frye's *Anatomy of Criticism* and Richard Chase's *The Quest for Myth* are among the finest of these studies.

Next to this feverishly active use of mythical parallels which has reoriented not only the novel and poetry but also literary criticism the retelling of classical legends by a Gide, a Sartre, or an Anouilh seems unimaginative and mild indeed. Gide has called on the Theseus myth to write a quasi confessional in the form of a novelette; Sartre has slightly revised the Orestes legend to assert his philosophy of responsible action and independence in play form; Anouilh has made the Antigone drama into a veiled protest against the Nazi occupation of France. In each instance the Greek original is displaced considerably in emphasis, without any substantial alteration in the subject matter of the legend. The characters usually retain their Greek names and identities and perform their classical functions. These works are mainly dramatic: even a writer like Gide, who has written fiction in *Thésée* and *Le Prométhée mal enchaîné*, reinterprets Oedipus in play form.

It would seem from the two categories briefly outlined that Jean Giraudoux belongs to the second, the less inventive. He too prefers drama for his mythic revivals although he uses the novella on at least one occasion with *Elpénor*. Almost every history of modern drama places his Greek plays alongside Sartre's *Les Mouches*, Gide's *Oedipe*, Anouilh's *Antigone, Eurydice*, and *Médée*, and Cocteau's *La Machine infernale, Antigone*, and *Orphée*. Two of his plays, *Electre* and *Amphitryon 38*, use material which dates from Aeschylus and Hesiod respectively and which has been used repeatedly in dramatic form ever since.

All of this makes us think that Giraudoux's classical revivals are part of the writer's awareness of tradition and his anxiety to emulate it in modern terms. Yet a closer examination of his work, both dramatic and fictional, reveals something of the heretic who is not only willing to tamper with the legend but also on occasions quite eager to render it in caricature. René Marill Albérès has already suggested this trait in Giraudoux: "Comme *Elpénor, Judith* et *Amphitryon 38* présentent la légende comme une formalité, un déroulement prévu de l'histoire avec lequel les hommes pourtant peuvent tricher."[1] Albérès also uses *pastiche irrespectueux* and *parodie* to express this tendency. It seems to be universally present in Giraudoux's works, almost as if his special contribution to modern literature were a systematic attempt to ridicule its most sacrosanct beliefs.

One can say that the twentieth century's principal contribution to poetry is the continuation and extension of the Symbolist notion, its principal contribution to the novel are the various devices linked with

---

[1] René Marill Albérès, *Esthétique et morale chez Jean Giraudoux* (Paris, Nizet, 1957), p. 360.

interior monologue, and its principal contribution to play writing is the extensive revival of Greek themes. On one occasion or another Giraudoux has held each of these up to genial pastiche.

In Chapter 7 of *Suzanne et le Pacifique* Suzanne engages in a singularly irreverent monologue about three French Symbolists, Mallarmé, Rimbaud, and Claudel. She begins:

Je m'irritais surtout contre trois noms qui revenaient constamment entre Simon et ses amis, trois noms d'ailleurs flamboyants même pour les non initiés, et qu'ils se reprenaient l'un à l'autre de force ou doucement comme les jongleurs les torches dans les cirques . . .[2]

The role Suzanne has them play, as she conveniently filters their names rather than their achievements through her imagination, indicates a studied disregard of their importance to modern poetry. She frivolously gives them a place in her island paradise which is amusingly in conflict with the serious nature of their verse—which Suzanne is incidentally totally ignorant of:

. . . trois noms dont j'ignorais presque l'orthographe . . . Mallarmé, Claudel et Rimbaud. Je ne savais rien d'eux-mêmes, pas s'ils étaient vivants, et pas s'ils étaient morts; j'ignorais si le voisin que je heurterais dans les gares en prenant mon billet, dans les pâtisseries en mangeant des éclairs, jamais, hélas! ne serait plus, ou toujours pourrait être, ô bonheur, Mallarmé, Claudel ou Rimbaud. (p. 179)

Somehow the notion of finding these particular three poets in a railroad station or pastry shop is especially bizarre and unlikely. One sees Giraudoux's special brand of *pastiche irrespectueux* at work here. In his selection of Symbolists he also seems to have chosen judiciously: Mallarmé, chief practitioner of "la poésie pure"; Claudel, the most effective Symbolist dramatist; Rimbaud, the poet as "voyant."

His pastiche of interior monologue is even more daring. We find this

[2] Jean Giraudoux, *Suzanne et le Pacifique* (Paris, Emile-Paul Frères, 1922), pp. 178–179.

astonishing sentence in the fifth chapter of *Juliette au pays des hommes:* "Ce qui intriguait Paris en ce moment, ce n'était certes pas la mort, c'était le Monologue intérieur."[3] Giraudoux stops his novel and allows one of his characters, Lemançon, to conjure up his own interior monologue in an obvious parody of the method. The section is blocked off from the rest of the chapter and is entitled "Monologue intérieur." It begins with several words in Italian (*"Il perche della caduta del marco"*), a characteristic trait of such polyglot users of the method as Valery Larbaud and James Joyce, proceeds through a series of clipped sentences which are logically disoriented. Lemançon subjects himself to an interior monologue much as if he were forcing upon himself a hypnotic trance. Juliette's response to the acrobatics reinforces the sense of absurdity: "Ainsi il différait si peu des phrases que prononcent les vieillards qui parlent tout seuls" (p. 154). She even suggests, somewhat mockingly, the need for "un manuel du monologue intérieur." Just as one does not meet Symbolist poets in pastry shops so one does not induce interior monologues. Again Giraudoux is making fun of his contemporaries and of their sacred literary beliefs.

Finally, he engages in full-scale ridicule of the extensive revival of Greek themes in the theater and of the century's obsession with myth. Not only does he use classical subject matter in his plays but he also surrounds his fictional world with the kind of mythical props which we associate with Joyce and Eliot—in a caricatured recipe. Thus, to return to Gilbert Highet's categories, it becomes clear that Giraudoux is engaging in neither of the two tendencies in modern myth-making. He is not using the "mythical method" of a Joyce or an Eliot nor is he reviving Greek themes in the straightforward manner of an Anouilh or a Sartre. He ironically underscores myth with the same gentle touch which he used in his pastiches of Symbolist poets and interior monologue.

[3] Jean Giraudoux, *Juliette au pays des hommes* (Paris, Emile-Paul Frères, 1924), p. 149.

II

Some critics have pointed out the peculiarity of the Giraudoux title *La Guerre de Troie n'aura pas lieu*. It is misleading when one realizes that the Trojan War took place both in Homeric mythology and its imitators as well as in Giraudoux's play: at least the play ends on the positive note that it will take place despite the efforts of Hector to ward it off. Christopher Fry was probably displeased with both the length and awkwardness of Giraudoux's title as well as with its distortion of the facts when he translated it as *Tiger at the Gates*. In a sense, however, despite the pleasing and appropriate nature of the English title something of Giraudoux's special relation to Greek drama is lost in it. Giraudoux has fancifully turned both the Homeric situation and its participants inside out to extract human absurdity from what was originally olympian bliss.

He has done much the same thing in *Amphitryon 38*. A hasty first glance at the dramatis personae and at the number *38* in the title leads one to think that Giraudoux is performing a useful service to scholarship and tradition by writing the thirty-eighth in an impressive line of Amphitryon plays. Örjan Lindberger, however, seems to have caught something of the ironical intent of the title:

Giraudoux's title is obviously meant to show that he was conscious of the motif having been treated many times before he tackled it. It is typical of our times that he found it necessary to point out this fact. Among contemporary literary values, originality is counted one of the most important. The writer who takes up an old motif might therefore feel it incumbent upon him to disarm the critics, who might otherwise describe his work as an imitation. The most effective way of doing this is of course to say very frankly: I have imitated not one predecessor, but thirty-seven! [4]

Most commentators who have studied the Amphitryon legend have failed to arrive at the magical number of Giraudoux's title; they usually

[4] Örjan Lindberger, *The Transformations of Amphitryon* (Stockholm, Almquist & Wiksell, 1956), pp. 167–168.

dismiss it with a polite shrug of the shoulder.[5] It is especially difficult to authenticate because of the diverse forms the legend has assumed and because of the lost Greek versions and the medieval versions with the same basic situation but with different names and events. But it is not impossible, from what we know about Giraudoux, for him to have insisted on a precise numerical count with tongue in cheek. The forbidding length and severity of *La Guerre de Troie n'aura pas lieu* as a title could easily be of the same order as the scholarly calculation of thirty-eight Amphitryons—each with the intention to dupe or at least to mislead.

The myth itself, we are told, dates back at least as far as Hesiod's *Theogony* and *Aspis* and the eleventh book of Homer's *Odyssey*. Örjan Lindberger, Hansres Jacobi, and Karl von Reinhardstoettner have already treated the individual Amphitryon versions in admirable detail. We might, however, make some judgments on the significance of the

---

[5] Örjan Lindberger's excellent *The Transformations of Amphitryon* is the most complete study of the myth. Hansres Jacobi's *Amphitryon in Frankreich und Deutschland* (Zürich, Juris-Verlag, 1952) studies the legend and its transformations mainly in France and Germany but does offer essential classical background. Jacobi is probably the first to feel that Giraudoux's ironical treatment helped destroy the legend. The first section of Part II of Karl von Reinhardstoettner's *Plautus: Spätere Bearbeitungen plautinischer Lustspiele* (Leipzig, W. Friedrich, 1886) is still a classic in the field of Amphitryon research, and several critics have insisted that Giraudoux was well acquainted with it; Reinhardstoettner's work, unfortunately, was written too early to account for Giraudoux's *Amphitryon 38* or Georg Kaiser's *Zweimal Amphitryon*. Articles on various aspects of the legend have appeared in German, Italian, French, and English. The most popular couplings of Giraudoux's version are with Kleist's and Molière's. Two excellent articles connect him with the German writer: J.-J. Anstett's "Jean Giraudoux et H. von Kleist," *Les Langues modernes*, Vol. 42 (1948), pp. 385–393 and L. Mazzoli's "Kleist e Giraudoux ultimi interpreti del mito di Anfitrione," *Dioniso*, Vol. 16 (1953), pp. 142–174. See also in the Kleist connection Laurent Lesage's *Jean Giraudoux, Surrealism, and the German Romantic Ideal* (Urbana, Illinois, University of Illinois Press, 1952) especially pp. 35–36, and Jacques Voisine's *Trois "Amphitryons" Modernes (Kleist, Henzen, Giraudoux)*, (Paris, Lettres Modernes, 1961, Archive No. 35). H. Petriconi's "Molières 'Amphitryon' und 'Amphitryon 38' von Jean Giraudoux," *Die neueren Sprachen*, Vol. 39 (1931), pp. 143–152, treats the Molière connection.

myth as a literary theme. The label "universal" is perhaps most appropriate. According to Lindberger, it seems to have invaded every major tradition in western literature except for the Spanish. Its beginnings correspond with the earliest phases of Greek literature and its most recent manifestation is in Georg Kaiser's *Zweimal Amphitryon,* which had its opening in Zürich in 1944.

The motif has probably attracted much enthusiasm because its subject matter lends itself appropriately to the gratification of the egocentric universe. Man flatters himself as being at the center of things when he reads of Jupiter's assuming human form for a brief period to seduce Alcmena. Jupiter succeeds only when he adopts the guise of a human being, Amphitryon, Alcmena's husband; when he hints at his real identity he is given no encouragement. All of the characters readily assume symbolic form: Alcmena is the untiringly faithful wife, Amphitryon the dedicated warrior, and Jupiter the encroaching deity. It is the god who is unduly lustful, the mortal who exhibits uncanny restraint. When the adulterous Jupiter violates the Biblical commandment, the unsuspecting Alcmena is entirely freed from guilt.

One of the more pleasing aspects of the legend is that it does not force the writer into the labyrinthine paths of moral judgment. The juxtaposition of gods and human beings, occupying the same plane, defies any kind of moralizing and sermonizing. Jupiter allows himself one extended night of frivolity. He only temporarily disrupts a blissful marriage—with no permanent ill effects. The assumption at the end of almost all of the Amphitryon versions is that Alcmena and her husband will be able to resume their marriage at the point it was interrupted by the appearance of Jupiter, a *deus ex machina* in the literal sense.

The legend has attracted playwrights almost exclusively. The impressive list includes Plautus, Rotrou, Molière, Dryden, Thomas Heywood, Kleist, Giraudoux, and Georg Kaiser. The medieval variations on the legend have managed somewhat to Christianize the myth without letting it lose its essential identity. Each writer seems to emphasize his peculiar dramatic bias in exploiting the legend. Plautus, who has created in the theater a comic tradition which thrives on duplicity, on the "double," has managed to build on the failure to distinguish between identicals. Molière has conveniently shifted focus, Lindberger tells us, to bring to the fore his favorite theme of courtly intrigue through a skillful series of mirror analogues: Jupiter equals Louis XIV; Amphitryon equals the Marquis de Montespan. Dryden uses the myth as a vehicle for Restoration comedy. Kleist was the first to remove the play from the Plautine-inspired tragicomedy and add a serious dimension of Germanic self-probing; his Alcmena gradually wears herself out psychologically. Georg Kaiser insists on the warrior's (Amphitryon's) neglect of his wife and has turned the myth into an antiwar play. This brief review offers further evidence of the "universal" possibilities of a legend which can accommodate the Virgin birth as readily as courtly intrigue.

Giraudoux has also found in the legend his accustomed tone and literary pace. His feeling for pastiche is amply rewarded. He has managed to puncture a myth by removing its Homeric distance and replacing it with the contemporaneity of a Noel Coward comedy. *Amphitryon 38* is as much a mockery of myth as Lemançon's and Suzanne's interludes were mockeries of interior monologue and Symbolist poetry. But the means employed are less obvious.

As various critics have pointed out, Alcmena is at the center of Giraudoux's play more obviously than in any other Amphitryon version. Gunnar Høst even suggests a new title: ". . . à dire vrai, Giraudoux n'a pas fait un *Amphitryon 38*, mais une *Alcmène première*." [6] In the first act Jupiter rehearses with Mercury his role as human lover. He is anxious to get the proper tone in his remarks so that he is convincingly Amphitryonic not only in appearance but in word and gesture. He is more of the performer, has a clearer sense of the paradoxical role of the actor, than any previous Jupiter. (The Am-

[6] Gunnar Høst, *L'Oeuvre de Jean Giraudoux* (Oslo, H. Aschehoug, 1942), p. 70.

phitryon tradition from Plautus through Kleist does not allow for this leisurely dress rehearsal.) In short, he wants to convince Alcmena by his every gesture not only that he is her husband Amphitryon (as in the previous versions) but that he is human. Giraudoux gives Jupiter an especially ironical speech, probably the most frequently quoted in the play, which convinces Mercury that he has mastered his role:

Ce ciel, je pense qu'il est à moi, et beaucoup plus depuis que je suis mortel que lorsque j'étais Jupiter! Et ce système solaire, je pense qu'il est bien petit, et la terre immense, et je me sens soudain plus beau qu'Apollon, plus brave et plus capable d'exploits amoureux que Mars, et pour la première fois, je me crois, je me vois, je me sens vraiment maître des dieux.[7]

It is clear that Giraudoux's intention in all this is to narrow the gap between divine and human. Myth is generally applied to subject matter as a way of elevating it or rendering it more universal. *Amphitryon 38,* on the contrary, turns an established myth into something more earthy and ephemeral. Jupiter's behavior especially seems to have all the human weaknesses. It is he, in Giraudoux's version, who starts a minor skirmish between two previously friendly nations merely to spirit Amphitryon away from his wife. No earlier Amphitryon play had dared puncture Jupiter's divinity by making the war subject to his caprice.

The second act is all Alcmena. We watch her clever verbal parries disarm Jupiter at every turn. She forces Jupiter, finally, into the one supreme compliment: "C'est que tu es le premier être vraiment humain que je rencontre . . ." (p. 62). The word "humain" is then the key word in this process of transforming Jupiter from god to man as he slowly loses his olympian presence. In the first act we observed Jupiter going to extraordinary lengths to impersonate a human. In the second act, after a

[7] *Le Théâtre Complet de Jean Giraudoux* (Neuchâtel et Paris, Ides et Calendes, 1945), Vol. 3, p. 43.

chastening night spent with Alcmena, he is all too ready to become human. In his first long speech to Mercury after he leaves Alcmena he insists on the virtues of this newly discovered state:

Mercure, l'humanité n'est pas ce que pensent les dieux! Nous croyons que les hommes sont une dérision de notre nature. Le spectacle de leur orgueil est si réjouissant, que nous leur avons fait croire qu'un conflit sévit entre les dieux et eux-mêmes. Nous avons pris une énorme peine à leur imposer l'usage du feu, pour qu'ils croient nous l'avoir volé; à dessiner sur leur ingrate matière cérébrale des volutes compliquées pour qu'ils inventent le tissage, la roue dentée, l'huile d'olive, et s'imaginent avoir conquis sur nous ces ôtages . . . Or, ce conflit existe, et j'en suis aujourd'hui la victime. (p. 67)

Jupiter's new position on the importance of being human is not only a distinct addition to the Amphitryon myth but the first step in Giraudoux's *pastiche irrespectueux*.

Giraudoux is not the first to bring new characters to the legend. Dryden had already superposed the world of Restoration comedy on the Amphitryon story—with a Mrs. Bracegirdle pronouncing the Prologue, Judge Gripus introducing in his own person, the corruption of the English legal system, and Phaedra (not to be confused with the tragic character in Euripides, Seneca, Racine, and D'Annunzio) representing the servant-girl type of Wycherley and Molière presuming to a position beyond her birth. Molière substituted Cléanthis for the Bromia of the original legend. The medieval Christians improvised at will, changing names and introducing new figures. Giraudoux's introduction of Leda in the second act, however, radically alters the legend. Jupiter had turned himself into a swan to gratify Leda; he had made the kind of metamorphosis which only a god is capable of. By placing Alcmena and Leda side by side, by compounding two myths, Giraudoux adds to the travesty. He brings back a figure from Jupiter's past to represent the period when he was content with being a god. Beside her is the unflinching Alcmena who is always ready, as Benjamin Crémieux has

said, "s'accepter mortelle et conjugale."[8] The conversation clearly favors
Alcmena in her defense of conjugal love.[9] (Earlier in the play when
Jupiter had insisted on an adjective to describe their night together
Alcmena had countered with unconscious irony, "conjugale.") A
peculiar substitution occurs with the myth taking on all the character-
istics of bedroom farce as the second act ends. Leda, disguised as
Alcmena, awaits, offstage, an Amphitryon whom she believes to be
Jupiter. This is Giraudoux's peculiar invention and seems to make sport
of the Plautine comedy of mistaken identity.

The final act serves to clear up the numerous complications, mostly
for the benefit of the audience, as both Alcmena and Amphitryon
remain blissfully ignorant of their respective infidelities. Jupiter's
reluctance to return to his position on Mt. Olympus is evidenced by his
increasing devotion to Alcmena and his willingness to use human ploys
to conceal the adulterous acts. He accepts Alcmena's offer of friendship,
a concept which is totally new to him, and safeguards the human
concept of the "couple."[10] The humanization of Jupiter is complete.

One of the complaints made against the Amphitryon legend is that it
has offered very little possibility for change or experimentation. The
French critic Albert Thibaudet began an article curiously entitled
"Amphitryon 39" in this way: "Si le sujet d'Amphitryon a été traité,
comme le veut le numérotage de Jean Giraudoux, trente-huit fois,
aucun des trente-sept successeurs d'Archippos, qui paraît avoir créé le

[8] Benjamin Crémieux, "Amphitryon 38, par Jean Giraudoux, à la Comédie
des Champs-Elysées," Nouvelle Revue française, Vol. 34 (1930), p. 139.

[9] See Georges May, "Marriage vs. Love in the World of Giraudoux," Yale
French Studies, No. 11, pp. 106–115.

[10] The problem of the "couple" is one of the themes which runs through
Giraudoux's theater. It is especially important in his quasi-Biblical Sodome et
Gomorrhe. Most of his commentators have discussed it. See, for example,
Georges May's "Marriage vs. Love in the World of Giraudoux"; André Dumas'
"Giraudoux ou la tragédie du couple," Esprit, No. 226 (1955), pp. 759–777; and
Laurent LeSage's Jean Giraudoux: His Life and Works (University Park,
Pennsylvania State University Press, 1959).

thème, n'a rien changé au fond de la comédie . . ." [11] With the exception of Giraudoux's play Thibaudet appears to be right. The slight twists and turns in the legend have never produced a genuine transformation in any of the characters or in the basic situation. There is nothing quite so astonishingly different between Plautus' and Molière's Alcmena or Dryden's and Rotrou's Jupiter as there is between Tirso de Molina's and Byron's Don Juan, for example. When Byron takes over the legendary lover and seducer he transforms him into the naive, seduced one.

Giraudoux plays the Byronic role with the Amphitryon myth. He is tampering with a legend, however, of considerably more antiquity and tradition than Don Juan. He has taken various set pieces, which had survived virtually intact between Plautus and Kleist, and engaged in a bit of what Donald Inskip has appropriately called "psychological juggling." [12] A Jupiter delighted with a wrinkle which he seems to have acquired from a night with Alcmena is a far cry from the Greek master of Olympus. An Alcmena with a sense of humor and a developed feeling for the paradoxical is very different from her unspirited namesake in Plautus and Dryden.

Indeed Giraudoux has so reshaped the myth that its most delightful moments are drawing-room interchanges between Jupiter and Alcmena. (Most reviewers have commented on the suitability of the Lunts in these two roles in the American adaptation which opened at the Schubert Theatre November 2, 1937. According to Donald Inskip, "Giraudoux himself had felt that Lunt's performance revealed another facet of the play, possibly more satisfying than what had been seen in Paris.") [13] In this respect *Amphitryon 38* begs comparison with Eliot's *The Cocktail Party,* which makes an oblique reference back to Euripides' *Alcestis* but only through the distorted optics of modern

---

[11] Albert Thibaudet, *"Amphitryon 39," Revue de Paris,* Vol. 44 (1937), p. 22.
[12] Donald Inskip, *Jean Giraudoux: The Making of a Dramatist* (Oxford, New York, Toronto, Oxford University Press, 1958), p. 61.
[13] *Ibid.,* p. 161.

psychology. But the seriousness of Eliot's application of the Greek myths to his plays is absent in Giraudoux, who favors the light touch. Eliot seems always intent on disguising the Greek origins of his plays in his titles: *The Family Reunion* (*Oresteia*), *The Cocktail Party* (*Alcestis*), *The Confidential Clerk* (*Ion*), *The Elder Statesman* (*Oedipus at Colonus*).[14] Giraudoux willfully admits his sources in his titles; any distortion he makes is usually in the direction of irony or satire.

Myth has then suffered a serious jolt in *Amphitryon 38*. The nostalgia for the human and ephemeral has replaced the accustomed emphasis of the legend. The best explanation for what Giraudoux has done here is probably to be found in his novella *Elpénor*—the title of which indicates immediately the shift from the godlike Ulysses to the most limited and fallible of the Greek warriors who survived the Trojan War.[15] Giraudoux improvises at will in this work to give the most unheroic possible view of the return from Troy. The description of Elpenor is possible only in a book which actively parodies myth:

For the sailor Elpenor was merely a specimen and symbol of all the thousands of ignorant and anonymous men who form the canvas on which an illustrious age is painted. Of all those famous heroes and their tremendous exploits he had approached only the most despised portions, recognizing Achilles from the way he stooped to wipe the mud from his heel; knowing Ajax by the spittle which landed on his shoulder as he pulled at his oar in front of the son of Orkeus; identifying Circe by the ease with which she helped Eclissa clean the carding-combs. The day Troy fell, Elpenor was polishing Hecuba's washtubs.[16]

---

[14] See Rudd Fleming, "*The Elder Statesman* and Eliot's 'Programme for the Métier of Poetry'," *Wisconsin Studies in Contemporary Literature*, Vol. 2 (1961), pp. 54–64.

[15] Giraudoux uses as his epigraph to *Elpénor* the following passage from Book X of Homer's *Odyssey:* "So died Elpenor, the youngest of us all. And his name shall not be spoken again, for he was neither valiant in war, nor steadfast in mind."

[16] *Elpénor*, translated from the French by Richard Howard with the assistance of Renaud Bruce (New York, Noonday Press, 1958), p. 94

Elpenor belongs with the Jupiter who boasts of his wrinkle and willingly accepts Alcmena in "friendship," with the Suzanne who remakes Claudel, Rimbaud, and Mallarmé into her own distorted view of them, with the Juliette who suggests the need for a manual of interior monologue. This is a world which thrives on genial pastiche and slightly irreverent mockery.

The final element of the Amphitryon myth which Giraudoux has seriously displaced is the Plautine confusion of identities. The legend came down to him with a built-in confusion between Sosia (Amphitryon's servant) and Mercury disguised to look like him. (This was so essential a part of the original plot that Rotrou, for example, called his play *Les Sosies*.) Giraudoux has diminished the role of Sosia, avoided the confrontation between Sosia and the neo-Sosia (Mercury); he has eliminated the stock comic situation in favor of a more complicated network of mistaken identity. A husband and wife, paradoxically, are able to face each other at the end of the play, each having committed adultery, neither being aware of it. There are none of the tedious rituals of identification between two Sosias and two Amphitryons, which Plautus and Dryden—with very different conceptions of the theater than Giraudoux—have forced on their audiences. The spectator plays his own special role in the proceedings as Jacques Houlet has skillfully pointed out: "Ce divertissement perpétuel de l'auteur qui n'est pas dupe, secrètement de connivence avec le spectateur contre le personnage, est un des charmes de Giraudoux." [17] Giraudoux has not eliminated the *Menaechmi-Comedy of Errors* confusion between "look-alikes" because of his failure to respond to the double motif. Indeed he uses it effectively in both *Judith* and *Elpénor*.[18] It is rather that Giraudoux is more anxious to humanize Jupiter than to show him off in a series of

[17] Jacques Houlet, *Le Théâtre de Jean Giraudoux* (Paris, Ardent, 1945), p. 181.
[18] In *Judith*, we have the remark, "Deux Holopherne! Deux Judith! Que de doublures, aujourd'hui!" following a natural confusion between Judith and Suzanne and Egon passing himself for Holopherne. In *Elpénor* Ulysses shows considerable relief when he discovers that the young Cyclops is not his

confused-identity scenes with Amphitryon. The subplot of the two
Sosias would merely distract from the playwright's principal intention;
by eliminating it he has managed once again to tamper with the original
legend.

III

Most commentators on Giraudoux seem to have shied away from
detailed discussions of *Amphitryon 38*. Joseph Chiari has set the
accustomed tone when he dismisses the play as one of its author's
"exquisite pieces of fantasy." [19] Such excellent recent studies of the
modern French theater as David Grossvogel's *The Self-Conscious Stage
in Modern French Drama* and Jacques Guicharnaud's *Modern French
Theatre from Giraudoux to Beckett* tend to concentrate on other
Giraudoux offerings. When *Tulane Drama Review* devoted an entire
issue to Giraudoux in 1959 none of the articles was limited exclusively to
Amphitryon 38 and only Wallace Fowlie in his admirable "Giraudoux'
Approach to Tragedy" gave the play more than passing recognition.
The best place to find lengthy studies on the work is in the criticism
devoted to the Amphitryon myth by Lindberger, Jacobi, Franz Stoessl,
and others. Most interesting of all is the excitement which the legend
and Giraudoux's interpretation of it has engendered among his literary
contemporaries: Thomas Mann has written on the myth proper and
Colette and Gabriel Marcel have written particularly on *Amphitryon
38*. [20] All of this would make us think that the play is easily dismissed as
an essential part of the Giraudoux canon and assumes its importance as

---

"double": "Every man quailed at the sight but Ulysses, who had feared much
more to find another Ulysses, even one of the same dimensions, than merely
another monster." Robert Brasillach calls this "le mythe du miroir." See his
Portraits (Paris, Plon, 1935), pp. 152–155.

[19] Joseph Chiari, *The Contemporary French Theatre* (London, Rockliff,
1958), p. 114.

[20] See Thomas Mann, "Amphitryon: Eine Wiedereroberung," in *Forderung
des Tages* (Berlin, S. Fischer, 1930); Colette, *"Amphitryon 38," Journal*,
October 14, 1934; Gabriel Marcel, *"Amphitryon 38," Nouvelles Littéraires*, Feb-
ruary 14, 1957.

a latter-day variation on a Greek myth. Its appeal to other creative writers might be explained by a remark made by Claude-Edmonde Magny which applies especially well to *Amphitryon 38:* ". . . le monde de Giraudoux est l'exemple le plus parfait peut-être d'un univers entièrement créé par le langage . . ."[21]

The play we have considered is not in the main current of Giraudoux's work. It occupies a curious marginal position with those other products of perhaps too much self-conscious artistry, *Suzanne et le Pacifique* and *Juliette au pays des hommes.* Its *pastiche irrespectueux* of an established myth places it in that limbo between Greek Revival and Mythical Method. It mixes the modern and the classical in a way which would doubtless please a Thomas Mann or a Colette.

[21] Claude-Edmonde Magny, *Précieux Giraudoux* (Paris, Editions du Seuil, 1945), p. 75.

PART TWO

The Classical in Modern Religious Experience

❖❖❖

THE PLACE OF THE CLASSICS IN
T. S. ELIOT'S CHRISTIAN HUMANISM

By David J. De Laura

THE LIFELONG INVOLVEMENT of T. S. Eliot in classical antiquity—in the problem of literary tradition, in the dual classical and Christian origins of western civilization, in the "availability" of classical sources to the contemporary poet—marks his criticism at every stage, and is everywhere implicitly present in the poetry and plays. And although Eliot deprecates his own classical scholarship, including himself among "those who . . . have not remembered enough to read the originals with ease" (*CML*, 25),* a contemporary classicist has noted that the range

---

* The following abbreviations have been used throughout in citing Eliot's works:

ASG: After Strange Gods: A Primer of Modern Heresy (New York, Harcourt, Brace and Co., 1934).

CML: The Classics and the Man of Letters (London, Oxford University Press, 1942).

CPP: The Complete Poems and Plays, 1909–1950 (New York, Harcourt, Brace and Co., 1952).

EAM: Essays Ancient and Modern (London, Faber and Faber, Ltd., 1936).

ICS: The Idea of a Christian Society (New York, Harcourt, Brace and Co., 1940).

NDC: Notes towards the Definition of Culture (London, Faber and Faber, 1948).

OPP: On Poetry and Poets (London, Faber and Faber, 1957).

SE: Selected Essays (3rd ed.; London, Faber and Faber, 1951).

SW: The Sacred Wood: Essays on Poetry and Criticism (3rd ed.; London, Methuen & Co., Ltd., 1932).

and subtlety of Eliot's classical borrowings and echoes ("this canaliza-
tion of tradition to generate charges of meaning"), as well as his
sensitivity to linguistic and textual matters, argue "an intimate and
learned acquaintance with the ancient classics."[1] Interestingly, Eliot's
incidental references to the Latin and Greek classics are considerably
more numerous in Selected Essays, where the latest piece is dated 1936,
than in On Poetry and Poets, which brings Eliot's output down to the
year 1956. In that earlier volume Eliot moved with agility and assurance
through wide fields of classical literature, not only invoking such
expected figures as Aeschylus, Aristophanes, Catullus, Cicero, Demos-
thenes, Euripides, Homer, Horace, Lucretius, Marcus Aurelius, Ovid,
Pindar, Plato, Sappho, Sophocles, Tacitus, Thucydides, and Virgil, but
also showing a sophisticated knowledge of the Greek Anthology,
Herondas, Lucian, Martial, Menander, Petronius, Propertius, Seneca,
and the Shepherd of Hermes.[2] The more recent collection contains
perfunctory references once again to Aeschylus, Catullus, Homer,
Lucretius, Propertius, Sappho, and Sophocles, and shows an extension
of interests to include Lactantius and the Pervigilium Veneris; but there
is nothing in the later Eliot to match the discriminating and exact
knowledge he displayed in the two essays on Seneca of 1927, unless
it be the far more generalized recent statements concerning Virgil in
"What is a Classic?" (1944) and "Virgil and the Christian World"
(1951).

These later essays, moreover, are a function of Eliot's growing
concern, through the years, with larger problems of society, a concern
which marks a retreat, one is tempted to say, from literary criticism.

---

[1] W. F. J. Knight, "T. S. Eliot as a Classical Scholar," in T. S. Eliot: A
Symposium for his Seventieth Birthday, ed. Neville Braybrooke (New York,
Farrar, Straus, & Cudahy, 1958), pp. 119 ff.

[2] In Eliot's Dante essay of 1920, which appeared in The Sacred Wood but was
not reprinted in Selected Essays, he discusses with balance and knowledge the
philosophical and literary characteristics of Parmenides, Empedocles, Heraclitus,
Zeno, Anaxagoras, and Democritus (SW, 119–120).

The high-water mark of his easy knowledgeability concerning the classics comes in the twenties. In the essays in *The Sacred Wood* (1920) Eliot has not yet displayed his interest in the Christian and classical sources of European culture and civilization, nor does his prose yet reveal the apocalyptic concern for the collapse of that civilization which his poetry of this period was clearly reflecting. Only the famous "Tradition and the Individual Talent" (1917) and his note on "Euripides and Professor Murray" (1920) concern the classics in any direct way. Presumably Eliot's conversion to Anglo-Catholicism sometime after the first world war accounts for the steadily mounting importance of the Christian-classical link, as well as of the apocalyptic note, in the prose from the twenties onwards. The events surrounding the first world war seem to have evoked from Eliot a poetry filled with the menace of a declining West, whereas the events of the years *entre les deux guerres* and, above all, of the second world war, moved him, now the celebrated man of letters, to become a serious religious and social critic, openly speaking for the maintenance of tradition and civilized standards in the face of an engulfing barbarism, while his poetry and drama were steadily progressing, in a new serenity, to uplands of the spirit where personal and social relations could be cultivated and, in some degree, protected from the collapse of standards in the world at large.

From the beginning, at any rate, Eliot displays, if not a scholar's, at least an unusually well-informed and independent layman's knowledge of the direction of contemporary classical studies. In 1920, in his devastating study of the late Gilbert Murray's translation of Euripides, he notes acidly that "we have a curious Freudian-social-mystical-rationalistic-higher-critical interpretation of the Classics and what used to be called the Scriptures" (*SE*, 62). But he admits that the work of the Cambridge school investigating the anthropological origins of Greek drama is "fascinating"; these "useful and important" studies, he finds, have sensibly affected our attitude towards the Classics; and it is this phase of classical study that Professor Murray—the friend and admirer of Miss Jane Harrison—represents. The Greek is no longer the awe-inspiring Belvedere of Winckelmann, Goethe, and Schopenhauer, the figure of which Walter Pater and Oscar Wilde offered us a slightly debased re-edition. And we realize better how different—not how much more Olympian—were the conditions of Greek civilization from ours; and at the same time Mr. Zimmern has shown us how the Greek dealt with analogous problems. Incidentally we do not believe that a good English prose style can be modelled upon Cicero, or Tacitus, or Thucydides. If Pindar bores us, we admit it: we are not certain that Sappho was *very* much greater than Catullus; we hold various opinions about Virgil; and we think more highly of Petronius than our grandfathers did. (*SE*, 63)

This realistic appraisal of the limits of classical taste in our times—with its post-Victorian refusal to exalt Periclean culture, and its implied interest in late Roman culture—offers us a handle by which to apprehend Eliot's complex relation to Graeco-Roman culture in the prose writings.

Concerning the criticism, Professor Wellek may be correct in saying that "Eliot's admiration for the Greek and Roman classics seems often quite general and theoretical,"[3] and certainly the rather large list of classical authors mentioned above does not necessarily imply any profound acquaintance with classical literature—for the depth and subtlety of Eliot's knowledge of the classics, the poetry and the plays are a surer proof. But Eliot's abiding interest in classical antiquity, as an indispensable element of the "tradition" he has attempted to define throughout his career and quite apart from the specifically Christian humanism which he has advocated in more recent years, is abundantly clear in the critical writings. The literary tradition Eliot proposed as early as 1917, in "Tradition and the Individual Talent," involved for the

[3] René Wellek, "The Criticism of T. S. Eliot," *The Sewanee Review*, LXVI (Summer, 1956), 429.

poet "the historical sense" and "a feeling that the whole of the literature of Europe from Homer and within it the whole of the literature of his own country, has a simultaneous existence and composes a simultaneous order" (*SE*, 14). The poet was called upon for an awareness "that the mind of Europe—the mind of his own country . . . is a mind which changes, and that this change is a development which abandons nothing *en route*" (*SE*, 16).[4] Eliot's Goethean and Arnoldian concern for the totality and unity of European culture was evident even in 1920, when he noted that the classics had, since the late nineteenth century, "lost their place as a pillar of the social and political system—such as the Established Church still is" (*SE*, 60), a linkage to be taken up and expanded within a few years. If the classics, he continues, are "to survive, to justify themselves as literature, as an element in the European mind, as the foundation for the literature we hope to create, they are very badly in need of persons capable of expounding them." This can be read as almost a program of Eliot's own later work, suggesting the classical foundations of his poetry as well as his critical concern for the continuity of European culture. Although Eliot's concern is not often with the quality of high Greek culture, he can enthusiastically define that quality in terms that recall his celebrated discussion of Metaphysical poetry: "Behind the dialogue of Greek drama we are always conscious of a concrete visual actuality, and behind that of a specific emotional actuality. . . . This is merely a particular case of the amazing unity of Greek, the unity of concrete and abstract in philosophy, the unity of thought and feeling, action and speculation, in

[4] Wellek judges, rather harshly, that Eliot "has a difficult and probably contradictory conception of history, development, and time and the poet's relation to it" (425–426), since Eliot sometimes seems to argue as if the poet were merely the mouthpiece of his age, whereas in the essay on "John Ford" (1932) Eliot argues for a timeless and universal art. Eliot, then, has "a double standard" (426–427). Concerning "Tradition and the Individual Talent," Wellek says: "Thus Eliot does not possess what has historically been called historical sense. He has no interest in historical causation, he is not a relativist, but rather understands that the absolute is in the relative; yet not finally and fully in it" (427).

life" (*SE*, 68).[5] More characteristically, perhaps, Eliot finds his favored poetic tone of the "alliance of levity and seriousness" to be common not only to Marvell and the other Metaphysicals, and to Gautier, Baudelaire, and Laforgue, but to Catullus, Propertius, and Ovid as well (*SE*, 296, 297). This pervasive wit in Marvell, we hear, "is more Latin, more refined, than anything that succeeded it"; "it is a quality of sophisticated literature" (*SE*, 301, 297). Thus the classics are already providing qualities applicable to the modern situation, an irregularly recurring literary syndrome (significantly derived from late Roman literature) which Eliot favors.

Nonetheless, Eliot's conception of the great tradition, especially as it has been embodied in "humanistic education" since the Renaissance, clearly takes the high achievements of classical culture as the key points of that tradition. In 1929, deploring the "desiccation of the study of philosophy in the universities," he found the fault to lie in "the teaching of philosophy to young men who have no background of *humanistic* education, the teaching of Plato and Aristotle to youths who know no Greek and are completely ignorant of ancient history" (*SE*, 486). In a similar pragmatic vein he noted in 1943, "The advantage of the study of Greek history and Greek political theory, as a preliminary to the study of other history and other theory, is its *manageability*: it has to do with a smaller area, with men rather than masses, and with the human

---

[5] This was in 1927; in 1921, in the essay on "The Metaphysical Poets," Eliot had spoken of the unified sensibility of the later Elizabethan and early Jacobean poets: men like Jonson and Chapman "incorporated their erudition into their sensibility" (*SE*, 286). Similarly, "A thought to Donne was an experience; it modified his sensibility." One wonders whether Arnold's famous discussion of "imaginative reason" as the chief quality of the century of Greek poetry from 530 to 430 B.C. did not lie behind Eliot's remarks on "the unity of thought and feeling" in Greek culture. Speaking of Simonides, Pindar, Aeschylus, and Sophocles, Arnold says, "no other poets have lived so much by the imaginative reason; no other poets who have made their work so well balanced, no other poets, who have so well satisfied the thinking power, have so satisfied the religious sense." See "Pagan and Mediaeval Religious Sentiment," *Essays in Criticism: First Series* (London, 1895), pp. 221–222.

passions of individuals rather than with those vast impersonal forces which in our modern society are a necessary convenience of thought, and the study of which tends to obscure the study of human beings" (*NDC*, 88). Moreover, Eliot is convinced that in reading Sappho, for example, we can gain "the experience which is the same for all human beings of different centuries and languages capable of enjoying poetry, the spark which can leap across those 2,500 years" (*OPP*, 117).

And yet we must not conceive that Eliot exalts the Greek inheritance over the Latin, in the manner of the German Hellenists, as if Greece were the source undefiled to which we must go directly. As Eliot makes clear in "What is a Classic?" (1944):

European literature is a whole, the several members of which cannot flourish, if the same blood-stream does not circulate throughout the whole body. The blood-stream of European literature is Latin and Greek—not as two systems of circulation, but one, for it is through Rome that our parentage in Greece must be traced. What common measure of excellence have we in literature, among our several languages, which is not the classical measure? What mutual intelligibility can we hope to preserve, except in our common heritage of thought and feeling in these two languages, for the understanding of which, no European people is in any position of advantage over any other? (*OPP*, 69–70)

In fact, so far does Eliot tip the balance the other way, that Rome is seen as having a unique historical destiny in western culture. Eliot sketches out the qualities of the classics: "maturity of mind, maturity of manners, maturity of language and perfection of the common style" (*OPP*, 59),[6] and finds these qualities especially summed up in Virgil,

[6] The first quality, says Eliot, "needs history, and the consciousness of history," as well as "comprehensiveness" and "universality" (*OPP*, 61, 67), and "The Classic must, within its formal limitations, express the maximum possible of the whole range of feeling which represents the character of the people who speak that language" (*OPP*, 67). Again, one detects the parentage of Arnold in some of these ideas. As Eliot found the classical qualities to be maturity of mind, manners, and language, so Arnold, in his Inaugural Lecture of 1857, found Periclean Athens adequately "modern" in qualities of mind ("the critical spirit")

whose comprehensiveness is "due to the unique position in our history of the Roman Empire and the Latin language: a position which may be said to conform to its *destiny*. . . . a unique destiny in relation to ourselves" (*OPP*, 67–68). Clearly, then, this is in many ways an assertion of a traditional classical humanism, and yet clearly too the modern classicist's willed assertions about the tradition can never be as unquestioning or taken for granted as, say, the attitudes of Pope. As D. E. S. Maxwell puts it, Eliot "questions tradition, makes demands of it, and asserts propositions about its nature that the earlier school did not"; moreover, not only do we detect a greater urgency in this more self-conscious acceptance of tradition, but it may also be Eliot's American origins which both give him perspective and make it impossible for him to accept the European tradition as a received body of expression.[7] Eliot is at great pains, in other words, to prove the efficacy and vitality and flexibility of classicism in a world of uncertain values where the place of the classics and of classical studies is by no means assured.[8]

---

and manners (external order, propriety of taste, refinement, simplicity, and toleration), and in the "adequacy" of its representation and interpretation of its age (the poetry of Pindar, Aeschylus, and Sophocles reflects "the highly developed human nature of that age"). See *Essays in Criticism: Third Series,* ed. Edward J. O'Brien (Boston, 1910), pp. 49 ff. Moreover, just as Eliot saw history and the consciousness of history as the mark of maturity of mind, so Arnold chose Thucydides as the example of the Greek "critical spirit," in his knowing "the true aim of history."

[7] See D. E. S. Maxwell, *The Poetry of T. S. Eliot* (London, Routledge & Paul, 1952), p. 24.

[8] Eliot found himself involved in the polemics surrounding the question of the place of classical studies in the schools. A reviewer ("T. I.") of Sir Richard Livingstone's *The Classics and National Life,* in *The New English Weekly,* XX (November 6, 1941), 22, had asked: "Is it possible even to the President of the Classical Association to believe that the national mind and national policy are or can ever be shaped by the infinitesimal fraction of the privileged few who can be taught the significance of Greek letters and Greek civilization?" Eliot replied (*Ibid.,* November 27, 1952) that "The real issue is between those who agree with Sir Richard Livingstone that some acquaintance with the intellectual and literary achievements of Greece is an essential element in a liberal education, and those

Eliot's concern for the classics and for the viability of the classical tradition is, in fact, precisely a function of his prolonged analysis of the modern condition. He has tried to define that condition, and in doing so his persistent exploration of the theme of cultural decay and collapse is unmistakable. That concern was obviously connected with Eliot's acute awareness of the limitations which the modern situation placed upon him or any artist; as he put it in 1933, "at the moment when one writes, one is what one is, and the damage of a lifetime, and of having been born into an unsettled society, cannot be repaired at the moment of composition" (*ASG,* 27). Here one is again reminded, as so often in Eliot, of the example of Matthew Arnold, who in the middle decades of the last century had calculated the cost and dangers of producing art in a society of unsettled beliefs, and later set about creating an intellectual and artistic climate favorable to the production of a high art. Eliot's own development of interests may be read as a similar movement from pessimistic analysis to at least a guarded hope for cultural regeneration. But the arc described by Eliot's developing concern with cultural collapse has, it must be admitted, been rather more unbrokenly somber-toned than Arnold's, a fact that has opened Eliot to the charges of doctrinaire liberals that he denies "the validity of life" and is the leader of "the army of reaction." But far from turning his back on "the general spectacle of civilization in decay," as Harold Laski has charged,[9]

---

who do not," and that once the implication of futile social pretension is taken away ("privileged few"), the answer to the reviewer's question is, "Why not?" Eliot sharply notes the implication in the reviewer's remarks "that Greek letters and Greek civilisation are insignificant" and his denial of "the value to society of all those values which can only be realised by an 'infinitesimal fraction'."

[9] See Harold J. Laski, in *T. S. Eliot: A Selected Critique,* ed. Leonard Unger (New York, Rinehart, 1948), pp. 36–37. Laski finds Eliot involved in a paradox (38): "the real effect of Mr. Eliot's work is to abandon the great mass of men and women to those who impose upon our civilization the very standards he is denouncing"; and he judges (42) Eliot's proposed Christian society to be "a technique of escape for a few chosen souls who cannot bear the general spectacle of civilization in decay." But even Laski admits that from this "degradation" Eliot, with "deep anxiety," "seeks to find a way out."

Eliot has indeed faced the collapse of traditional values in modern western civilization with almost unexampled honesty. Especially from the early thirties onward, we catch in his writings the note that our age is "one of progressive decline of civilization." He immediately adds: "This is a form of speculation in which I am not interested. There is a certain saving egotism . . . which prevents us from despair so long as we believe that there is anything that we can do which may possibly help to improve matters" (*EAM*, 131–132). But in fact from this time forward there is a growing apocalyptic tone in Eliot's writings, a prophetic strain which obviously jibed well with his Christian convictions. In 1931 we find him predicting, with what seems chilling complacency, the "collapse" of modern civilization and the "dark ages" which will follow:

The Universal Church is to-day, it seems to me, more definitely set against the World than at any time since pagan Rome. I do not mean that our times are particularly corrupt. I mean that Christianity, in spite of certain local appearances, is not, and cannot be, within measurable time, "official." The World is trying the experiment of attempting to form a civilized but non-Christian mentality. The experiment will fail; but we must be very patient in waiting its collapse; meanwhile redeeming the time: so that the Faith may be preserved alive through the dark ages before us; to renew and rebuild civilization, and save the World from suicide. (*SE*, 387)

The implied parallel between late Roman civilization and the twentieth century is, as we shall see, a frequent theme from this time onward.

The lineaments of the modern world were clear from the beginning. In 1923 Eliot spoke of modern materialism as issuing in "pure boredom," a condition of which the civilized world may well die (*SE*, 459). And in 1935 he defined secularism as "concern . . . only with changes of a temporal, material, and external nature," and sweepingly condemned "the whole of modern literature" for its inability to "understand the meaning of, the primacy of the supernatural over the natural life: of something which I assume to be our primary concern" (*SE*, 400, 398). But clearly the events leading to and surrounding the second world war presented a serious crisis in Eliot's own life and gave decisive impetus to his social and religious analysis of the disease of western civilization. Munich, Eliot reports, was the starting point for *The Idea of a Christian Society:*

I believe that there must be many persons who, like myself, were deeply shaken by the events of September 1938 in a way from which one does not recover; persons to whom that month brought a profounder realisation of a general plight. . . . The feeling which was new and unexpected was a feeling of humiliation, which seemed to demand an act of personal contrition, of humility, repentance and amendment. . . . It was not . . . a criticism of the government, but a doubt of the validity of a civilisation. (*ICS*, 64–65)

And so, though Eliot's general portrait of the twentieth century as "an age of uncertainty, an age in which men are bewildered by new sciences, an age in which so little can be taken for granted as common beliefs, assumptions and background of all readers" (*OPP*, 114), remains substantially the same, his analysis of the joint breakdown of the religious and the humanistic traditions—the two chief means in Eliot's view of ensuring common beliefs and assumptions—becomes more detailed in the later writings, especially in *Notes towards the Definition of Culture*, published at intervals between 1943 and 1948. Moreover, *Notes* sounds the apocalyptic tone even more urgently than the earlier works did: it is obviously much exercised by the ideas of "the gloom of our present position," "the general lowering of culture," and "cultural debility" (*NDC*, 40, 79, 80). And the effect of Eliot's remark, that we are "destroying our ancient edifices to make ready the ground upon which the barbarian nomads of the future will encamp in their mechanised caravans," is hardly blunted by his deprecatory disclaimer: "The previous paragraph is to be considered only as an incidental flourish to relieve the feelings of the writer and perhaps of his more sympathetic readers. It is no longer possible, as it might have been a hundred years ago, to find consolation in prophetic gloom" (*NDC*, 108). Eliot may decline the prophet's mantle and tailor his humility to the taste of the age, but the deepening gloom of his writings during and after the war years gave his prose career a sense of urgency and commitment which his earlier writings may have lacked.

The "ancient edifices" whose collapse Eliot rather dourly superintends are, plainly, the tradition of historical Christianity and that of a classical literary humanism. And the two are, as we shall see, in mysterious ways intertwined. Eliot's sense of culture oscillates disconcertingly between the modern sociological conception of the term and the older and more specialized belletristic sense; but if it is in that more general sense that he expresses his conviction "that our own period is one of decline; that the standards of culture are lower than they were fifty years ago" (*NDC,* 19), it is unquestionable that "culture" in its narrower educational meaning is what is often on Eliot's mind:

the culture of Europe has deteriorated visibly within the memory of many who are by no means the oldest among us. . . . For there is no doubt that in our headlong rush to educate everybody, we are lowering our standards, and more and more abandoning the study of those subjects by which the essentials of our culture—of that part of it which is transmissible by education—are transmitted. (*NDC,* 108)

No doubt this abandoned tradition makes up much of "Time's ruins" on which Burbank meditated, those "fragments" which the speaker in *The Waste Land* shored up against his ruins (*CPP,* 24, 50). In fact, traditional "wisdom" itself seems to have broken down, and its custodians to have played the conscious deceivers. As *Four Quartets* puts it:

> Had they deceived us
> Or deceived themselves, the quiet-voiced elders,
> Bequeathing us merely a receipt for deceit?
> The serenity only a deliberate hebetude,
> The wisdom only the knowledge of dead secrets

> Useless in the darkness into which they peered
> Or from which they turned their eyes. . . .
>   Do not let me hear
> Of the wisdom of old men, but rather of their folly,
> Their fear of fear and frenzy, their fear of possession,
> Of belonging to another, or to others, or to God.
> The only wisdom we can hope to acquire
> Is the wisdom of humility: humility is endless.
>   (*CPP*, 125–126)

Thus one version of inherited wisdom and culture is rejected, and precisely by religious standards. But, more commonly, Eliot's lament for the abandonment of the traditional humanistic sources of our culture is couched in much the same terms as those in which he discusses the breakdown of religious sensibility. As part of a discussion of the possibility that, in the decline of poetry written in minor languages, "people everywhere would cease to be able to express, and consequently be able to feel, the emotions of civilized beings," Eliot abruptly remarks:

Much has been said everywhere about the decline of religious belief; not so much notice has been taken of the decline of religious sensibility. The trouble of the modern age is not merely the inability to believe certain things about God and man which our forefathers believed, but the inability to *feel* towards God and man as they did. (*OPP*, 25)

Clearly, religious sensibility (presumably the foundation of belief) and our classical cultural inheritance are, in Eliot's view, transmitted by the same process.

Eliot's poetry is filled with reflections on history and historical process, and there is no cry more poignant than his question, "*When* will Time flow away?" (*CPP*, 91). But Eliot has faced the burden of history and has accepted the task of historical explanation, and nowhere more fully than in the matter of the decline of religious sensibility, which he habitually couples with the decline of civilization itself. Twice during

the twenties, in the course of discussing Shakespeare and his contemporaries, Eliot sought to link the Elizabethan attitude toward life, which
he saw as "one of anarchism, of dissolution, of decay" (SE, 116), to a
continuous though changing line of European sensibility derived from
antiquity. In 1924, he traced the attitude from Seneca to the twentieth
century (SE, 116–117), and three years later, in his much more ambitious "Shakespeare and the Stoicism of Seneca," he found this modern
attitude of "self-dramatization," ultimately derived from Seneca, in
both Shakespeare and Nietzsche. Apparently Roman stoicism has
fathered a philosophy of personal self-assertion and a refusal of authority external to the individual which is still as dominant in the
twentieth century as it was in late classical culture and in Elizabethan
England: "Stoicism is the refuge for the individual in an indifferent or
hostile world too big for him; it is the permanent substratum of a
number of versions of cheering oneself up. The stoical attitude is the
reverse of Christian humility" (SE, 131–132). Eliot daringly pushes back
his survey so as to include even Greek tragedy within the historically
realized arc of sensibility which he rejects:

The differences between the fatalism of Greek tragedy, and the fatalism of
Seneca's tragedies, and the fatalism of the Elizabethans, proceed by delicate
shades; there is continuity, and there is also a violent contrast, when we look
at them from far off. In Seneca, the Greek ethics is visible underneath the
Roman stoicism. In the Elizabethans, the Roman stoicism is visible beneath
the Renaissance anarchism. (SE, 133–134)

There is, no doubt, a certain exhilaration in this view of European
intellectual history "from far off," despite the tendentious and moralistic
tone Eliot adopts. And inevitably it is the present which Eliot, characteristically, wishes to illuminate. He includes Shakespeare in the line of
influential figures of the Renaissance who have bequeathed to us the
suspect cult of personality:

What influence the work of Seneca and Machiavelli and Montaigne seems to
me to exert in common in that time, and most conspicuously through

Shakespeare, is an influence towards a kind of self-consciousness that is new; the self-consciousness and self-dramatization of the Shakespearean hero. . . . Roman stoicism was in its own time a development in self-consciousness; taken up into Christianity, it broke loose again in the dissolution of the Renaissance. Nietzsche . . . is a late variant: his attitude is a kind of stoicism upside-down; for there is not much difference between identifying oneself with the Universe and identifying the Universe with oneself. (*SE*, 139– 140) [10]

This elaborate attempt at reconstructing a long-range view of one important aspect of European sensibility, a kind of *counter*-tradition to the one which Eliot most approves, clearly bears on his early critical views concerning impersonality and discipline in art, and on the rootless and fragmented personalities who people the early poems. But here we must consider Eliot's ambitious remarks as seminal in his continuing discussion of the collapse of the religious tradition in Europe, especially from the sixteenth century to the twentieth.

We are not surprised that Eliot reads the religious schisms of the sixteenth century as symptomatic of a general "disintegration of European culture" (*NDC*, 29). Similarly, he puts his discussion of the limitations of eighteenth-century religious sensibility in the context of the age's failure to grasp the "relatedness between two great cultures, and . . . their reconciliation under an all-embracing history" (*OPP*,

---

[10] In his 1932 essay on John Ford, Eliot disconcertingly seems to *exempt* the Elizabethans from the sense of "unsettlement and change" which is evident in Imperial Rome and in modern culture. He remarks: "In Elizabethan and Jacobean drama, and even in the comedy of Congreve and Wycherley, there is almost no analysis of the particular society of the times." He feels the Elizabethans and Jacobeans are "blessed" in lacking "this sense of a 'changing world,' of corruption and abuses peculiar to their time," whereas "the greater French novelists, from Stendhal to Proust, chronicle the rise, the regime, and the decay of the upper bourgeoisie in France" (*SE*, 202). Preoccupied here with a kind of "timeless" view of high art, Eliot declares that the Elizabethans, like Dante and the great Greek dramatists, could concentrate "upon the common characteristics of humanity in all ages, rather than upon the differences" (202–203), whereas "it was a changing world which met the eyes of Lucian or of Petronius" (203).

62)—in other words, precisely a failure of *cultural* vision. These limitations of religious outlook mark "the decay of a common belief and a common culture" (*OPP*, 61). Moreover, in his discussion of Baudelaire we find Eliot linking cultural "degradation" with the collapse of religious consciousness (*SE*, 427), stating as a general principle: "When religion is in a flourishing state, when the whole mind of society is moderately healthy and in order, there is an easy and natural association between religion and art" (*SE*, 440). He goes on to deplore the late nineteenth century's "blundering attempts" artificially to re-create that easy association in an age of "dissolution" (*SE*, 442–443). As for the present, Eliot has tried to gauge the degree to which western society may still accurately be described as Christian. He finds himself "surprised that the people retains as much Christianity as it does" (*ICS*, 28–29), and he refuses to take for granted the idea "that the division between Christians and non-Christians in this country is already, or is determined to become, so clear that it can be reduced to statistics" (*ICS*, 50). Convinced that we live in a "neutral society," but that the alternatives before us are a Christian society or a pagan society, Eliot challenges the idea that we have had a Christian society in the past, and that today we have a pagan society (*ICS*, 9). We have not yet, he explains, reached the point where Christians are "a minority . . . in a society which has ceased to be Christian," since society has not yet become "positively something else" (*ICS*, 10). On that very cautious note of hope he builds his view of the future.

Eliot's stance before the dominant modes of thought in the modern world is, then, a curious mixture of contempt, tolerance, and hope. If the regnant characteristics of the modern temper, in Eliot's historical view, are the apotheosis of personality and a kind of atomistic individualism, these qualities are most evident today in the complex of attitudes and institutions to which Eliot refers by the umbrella term, "liberalism." At any rate, liberalism seems a domesticated version of the classical stoicism he described in connection with the Elizabethans. Its teeth now drawn and its intentions consciously benevolent, liberalism is dangerous in its very negativeness; the worst that can be said of it is "that a negative element made to serve the purpose of a positive is objectionable" (*ICS*, 14). And thus Eliot, by reaction, is seeking "a way of life for a people," and the choice he sees is between "a pagan, and necessarily stunted culture, and a religious, and necessarily imperfect culture" (*ICS*, 15-16). Put otherwise, "the only alternative to a progressive and insidious adaptation to totalitarian worldliness for which the pace is already set, is to aim at a Christian society" (*ICS*, 18). But the vision of such a society recedes before a more imminent prospect of religion and culture in joint decay in the non-Christian society:

Anything like Christian traditions transmitted from generation to generation within the family must disappear, and the small body of Christians will consist entirely of adult recruits. . . . I am concerned with the dangers to the tolerated minority; and in the modern world, it may turn out that the most intolerable thing for Christians is to be tolerated. . . . We might, of course, merely sink into an apathetic decline: without faith, and therefore without faith in ourselves; without a philosophy of life, either Christian or pagan; and without art. Or we might get a "totalitarian democracy": . . . a state of affairs in which we shall have regimentation and conformity, without respect for the needs of the individual soul; the puritanism of hygienic morality in the interest of efficiency; uniformity of opinion through propaganda, and art only concerned when it flatters the official doctrines of the time. (*ICS*, 20–22)

One senses here the authenticity and some of the inflexibility of Eliot's views. Iris Murdoch finds in him "something of that 'Jansenism of temperament' which he attributes to Pascal." [11] Certainly one may agree that Eliot is inclined to neglect "the extent to which liberalism is entwined with our Christian tradition as it is in reality and as a working power now is." [12] The apocalyptic note in Eliot's politico-religious

[11] Iris Murdoch, in Braybrooke, *A Symposium*, pp. 157–158.
[12] *Ibid.*, p. 160. She finds Eliot neither in the English conservative tradition, nor in the Idealist tradition of flexible and concrete thinking: "He is an eclectic moralist" (157). She continues cogently: "our mixed-up modern world needs for

writings can scarcely be missed; the imaginative capacity for conveying the disastrous collapse of our whole tradition, classical and Christian, so striking and authoritatively present in the poetry, informs almost every aspect of his critical and social writings as well.

But if in Eliot's view the decline of modern civilization is the end of a special combination of factors, marked above all by the collapse of classical standards and of religious sensibility, the positive historical relationship of these two fountainheads of European civilization remains to some extent obscure and problematic. The theme of the double inheritance, however, is as persistent as any of Eliot's major concerns. As early as 1923 we find him refuting a fallacy of "popular ethnology and popular philology" to the effect that classical studies may be neglected in England because the French spirit is more akin to that of Rome than is the English. He replies with one of the first statements of his crucial view on the unity of European culture: "The fact is, of course, that *all* European civilisations are equally dependent upon Greece and Rome— so far as they are civilisations at all. . . . If everything derived from Rome were withdrawn—everything we have from Norman-French society, from the Church, from Humanism, from every channel direct and indirect, what would be left? . . . England is a 'Latin' country." [13] Most

---

its unravelling a type of sensitive 'concrete' understanding to which if we deny the name of thinking we are lost. . . . It is especially important now to keep alive such sources of moral response as remain to us. It seems to me that Mr. Eliot plays dangerously when he rejects *in toto* the moral content of liberalism and appeals over its head to a conception of dogma and authority which can itself play an ambivalent role. . . . It is at least perilous to neglect the remnants of that liberal moral absolutism which, without dogma, holds that there are certain things which cannot be done to human persons" (159).

[13] "The Classics in France—and in England," *The Criterion,* II (October, 1923), 104–105. Eliot's beginning interest here in "everything derived from Rome" may have been stimulated by Whitehead's article, "The Place of Classics in Education," which appeared several months earlier in the *Hibbert Journal,* XXI (January, 1923), 248–261. (It was to appear several years later in *The Aims of Education,* 1929.) Whitehead concluded: "The marvellous position of Rome in relation to Europe comes from the fact that it has transmitted to us a double inheritance. It received the Hebrew religious thought, and has passed on to Europe its fusion

of the key ideas are at least implied here already: the emphasis on classical studies, on European cultural unity, on Rome as the unique channel of human and divine knowledge—and, as a seed to be developed, on the role of the Church in supporting cultural unity. This latter theme is taken up in Eliot's 1929 review of E. K. Rand's *Founders of the Middle Ages,* in which Eliot reports that one of Rand's chief theses is "that the attitude of the Church towards classical culture was always double—an attitude of disapproval of pagan literature and learning was offset by one of pious preservation and enjoyment, so that Dr. Rand is able to insist upon the continuity of the classical tradition in Christianity."[14] The following year Eliot pursues the theme of "the continuity of pagan and Christian culture" apropos of the setting of Pater's *Marius,* speaking of "the intellectual activity which was then amalgamating Greek metaphysics with the tradition of Christ," though Eliot shows his first realization of the ambiguities involved when he observes that neither Pater nor Marius "seems to have any realization of the chasm to be leapt between the meditations of Aurelius and the Gospel" (*SE,* 441, 442). His emerging thesis is sharpened in focus in "Modern Education and the Classics" (1931), where he suggests "the fundamental defence of Latin and Greek":

There are two and only two finally tenable hypotheses about life: the Catholic and the materialistic. The defence of the study of the classical languages must ultimately rest upon their association with the former, as

---

with Greek civilisation. Rome itself stands for the impress of organisation and unity upon diverse fermenting elements. Roman law embodies the secret of Roman greatness in its Stoic respect for intimate rights of human nature within an iron framework of empire. Europe is always flying apart because of the diverse explosive character of its inheritance, and coming together because it can never shake off that impress of unity it has received from Rome. The history of Europe is the history of Rome curbing the Hebrew and the Greek, with their various impulses of religion, and of science, and of art, and of quest for material comfort, and of lust of domination, which are all at daggers drawn with each other. The vision of Rome is the vision of the unity of civilisation" (261).

[14] *Times Literary Supplement* (London), March 29, 1929, p. 200.

must the defence of the primacy of the contemplative over the active life.
... It is high time that the defence of the Classics should be dissociated from
objects which, however excellent under certain conditions and in a certain
environment, are of only relative importance—a traditional public-school
system, a traditional university system, a decaying social order—and
permanently associated where they belong, with something permanent: the
historical Christian Faith. (*SE*, 514)

Despite the sweeping terms in which this is put, the problem is still
fundamentally one of education, as Eliot explains:

I am here concerned with readers who are prepared to prefer a Christian
civilisation, if a choice is forced upon them; and it is only upon readers who
wish to see a Christian civilisation survive and develop that I am urging the
importance of the study of Latin and Greek. . . . And the only hope that
I can see for the study of Latin and Greek, in their proper place and for
the right reasons, lies in the revival and expansion of monastic teaching
orders. There are other reasons, and of the greatest weight, for desiring to
see a revival of the monastic life in its variety, but the maintenance of
Christian education is not the least. The first educational task of the
communities should be the preservation of education within the cloister,
uncontaminated by the deluge of barbarism outside. . . . As the world at
large becomes more completely secularized, the need becomes more urgent
that professedly Christian people should have a Christian education, which
should be an education both for this world and for the life of prayer in this
world. (*SE*, 515–516)

Thus, despite his disclaimers, Eliot does view the modern situation
metaphorically as a collapse analogous to the fall of Rome, and the
future as the dark ages to come. But the crucial question, that of the
precise relation of classical studies to Christianity, remained unan-
swered.

The coming of the war prompted Eliot to examine the question
further. It seems to be something like the "monastic" education
described by Eliot in 1932 which he was to prescribe for the Community
of Christians in *The Idea of a Christian Society,* that spiritual elite
which he defines as

not an organisation but a body of indefinite outline; composed of both clergy and laity, of the more conscious, more spiritually and intellectually developed of both. It will be their identity of belief and aspiration, their background of a common system of education and a common culture, which will enable them to influence and be influenced by each other, and collectively to form the conscious mind of the nation. (*ICS*, 43)

In 1942, in *The Classics and the Man of Letters*, Eliot declared this common education and culture necessary for the continuing identity of a unified European culture, a culture whose roots are Christianity and the classical languages. His ostensible thesis is "that the maintenance of classical education is essential to the maintenance of English Literature," a concern, then, not only for specialists, but for theologians, historians, the clergy and the ministry, teachers of modern languages and literature, and literary critics—and a process involving history, logic, and philosophy. But he concludes by greatly broadening his thesis, claiming that "the preservation of a living literature is more than a matter of interest only to amateurs of verse and readers of novels"; instead, those he appeals to will recognize it as a matter of

the preservation of developed speech, and of civilization against barbarism. They will be those who appreciate the need, if the present chaos is ever to be reduced to order, of something more than an administrative or economic unification—the need of a cultural unification in diversity of Europe, and who believe that a new unity can only grow on the old roots: the Christian faith, and the classical languages which Europeans inherit in common. These roots are, I think, inextricably intertwined. I should not care to risk the heresy, upon which some religious-political writers have appeared to verge, of regarding Christianity as a European, rather than a universal Faith: I do not wish to be accused of inventing a new heresy to the effect that salvation depends upon getting a first in classics. But the culture of Europe, including Britain, cannot preserve its intellectual vigour unless a high standard of Latin and Greek scholarship is maintained amongst its teachers. . . . I am quite aware that an educational system cannot of itself bring about either great faith or great literature. . . . But those who care for the preservation, the extension and advancement of our culture cannot fail to interest themselves . . . in our classical heritage. (*CML*, 26–27)

That "the advancement of our culture" is the advancement of a specifically *Christian* culture is even clearer in Eliot's 1946 lecture on "The Unity of European Culture," where he speaks of "the sources which we share in common: that is, the literature of Rome, of Greece and of Israel" (*NDC*, 113). "We have," he explains, "our common classics, of Greece and Rome; we have a common classic even in our several translations of the Bible" (*NDC*, 114). He goes on to call the amalgam our *Christian* heritage, indicating the centrality of the religious element in our culture:

> If Christianity goes, the whole of our culture goes. Then you must start painfully again, and you cannot put on a new culture ready made. . . . You must pass through many centuries of barbarism. . . .
> To our Christian heritage we owe many things beside[s] religious faith. Through it we trace the evolution of our arts, through it we have our conception of Roman law which has done so much to shape the Western World, through it we have our conceptions of private and public morality. And through it we have our common standards of literature, in the literatures of Greece and Rome. The Western World has its unity in this heritage, in Christianity and in the ancient civilisations of Greece, Rome and Israel, from which, owing to two thousand years of Christianity, we trace our descent. (NDC, 122–123)

For the most part, then, Eliot asserts the reconciliation of the two streams of European culture on a historical, *de facto* basis, and does not explore any deeper antagonisms which may persist between the two traditions. Only in the case of one classical figure does he more fully suggest the complex process by which classical values are subsumed in the Christian synthesis.

That figure is, of course, Virgil. In 1944 Eliot had spoken of Virgil as the one "who, as it was his function to lead Dante towards a vision he could never himself enjoy, led Europe towards the Christian culture which he could never know" (*OPP*, 70). This is the theme Eliot developed, seven years later, in "Virgil and the Christian World." The latter essay is Eliot's most extended treatment of a classical author, and the fact that his avowed chief concern is with "those characteristics of Virgil which render him peculiarly sympathetic to the Christian mind" (*OPP*, 121) suggests both the limitations of Eliot's classical sympathies and the note of cultural polemics which almost invariably enters into his discussion of the relation of the ancient world to Christianity. Eliot's essentially nonliterary interest in Virgil is clear in his admission that his peculiar interest in the ancient poet "is not to accord him any exaggerated value as a poet, or even as a moralist, above that of all other poets Greek and Roman," and in the fact that he takes his cue from Virgil's allegedly "prophetic" and "inspired" qualities in the fourth *Eclogue:*

> But what really concerns me is the element in Virgil which gives him a significant, a unique place, at the end of the pre-Christian and at the beginning of the Christian World. He looks both ways; he makes a liaison between the old world and the new, and of his peculiar position we may take the fourth *Eclogue* as a symbol. In what respects, therefore, does the greatest of Roman poets anticipate the Christian world in a way in which the Greek poets do not? . . . Virgil made of Roman civilization in his poetry something better than it really was. His sensibility is more nearly Christian than that of any other Roman or Greek poet: not like that of an early Christian perhaps, but like that of a Christianity from the time at which we can say that a Christian civilization had come into being. We cannot compare Homer and Virgil; but we can compare the civilization which Homer accepted with the civilization of Rome as refined by the sensibility of Virgil. (*OPP*, 123, 125)

The key words are *labor, pietas, fatum*. As for the first, the Greeks taught us the dignity of leisure and the supreme value of the life of contemplation, but Virgil affirmed the dignity of manual labor and thus enabled the Christian monastic orders to join the contemplative life and the life of agricultural labor. For Virgil, likewise, *pietas* "implies an attitude towards the individual, towards the family, towards the region, ...towards the impersonal destiny of Rome.... and towards the gods"; it therefore "implies a unity and an order" among these values: "it is in fact an attitude towards life" (*OPP*, 127). This *reverence* in Aeneas is "an analogue and foreshadow of Christian humility." *Fatum*, moreover, implies a sense of "destiny," which is above either necessitarianism or caprice: it is "an election which cannot be explained, a burden and responsibility rather than a reason for self-glorification" (*OPP*, 128). This destiny Virgil consciously saw as the *imperium romanum;* for him, it was "a worthy justification of history" (*OPP*, 129). Eliot concludes, "We are all, so far as we inherit the civilization of Europe, still citizens of the Roman empire"—though of course it was not the Roman empire of history: "It was something greater, but something which exists because Virgil imagined it. It remains an ideal, but one which Virgil passed on to Christianity to develop and to cherish" (*OPP*, 130).

At this point Eliot pauses to qualify his encomium, to define Virgil's inevitable shortcomings with regard to the Christian culture he anticipated. Eliot finds the role Dante assigned to Virgil, that of guide and teacher up to a point Virgil could not pass, as "an exact statement of Virgil's relation to the Christian world" (*OPP*, 130). When we have said the best that we can about Virgil—that his world, more than Homer's, approximates to a Christian world "in the choice, order and relationship of its values," and that "Virgil, among classical Latin poets or prose writers, is uniquely near to Christianity"—nonetheless, Virgil "just falls short" of deserving the phrase *anima naturaliter Christiana* (*OPP*, 130). He lacks the term *amor:* "Love is never given, to my mind, the same significance as a principle of order in the human soul, in society or in the universe that *pietas* is given; and it is not Love that causes *fatum,* or moves the sun and the stars" (*OPP*, 131). "Virgil," then, "was, among all authors of classical antiquity, one for whom the world made sense, for whom it had order and dignity, and for whom, as for no one before his time except the Hebrew prophets, history had meaning"; but he was denied Dante's vision of Love as the ordering principle of the universe (*OPP*, 131). This is one of the few places where Eliot suggests substantial limitations in his frequently reiterated thesis that "we are the common trustees" of "the legacy of Greece, Rome and Israel" (*NDC*, 124)—and obviously, as Eliot presents him, Virgil is by far the most susceptible to such treatment. We sense a kind of short circuit in Eliot's argumentation, a kind of stubborn refusal to get behind the essentially *historical* assertion about the reality of European culture to a judgment of metaphysical principles. As recently as 1955 we find Eliot once again declaring simply:

> The great poets of Greece and Rome, as well as the prophets of Israel, are the ancestors of Europe, rather than Europeans in the mediaeval and modern sense. It is because of our common background, in the literatures of Greece, Rome and Israel, that we can speak of "European literature" at all: and the survival of European literature, I may mention in passing, depends on our continued veneration of our ancestors. (*OPP*, 211)

Ostensibly, the interest is frequently literary; but behind it we sense the fear of the collapse of a whole complex world of values, and behind all is Eliot's essential commitment to the survival of Christianity as a force in the modern world. The question remains: What has the study of ancient literature and culture to do with "the prophets of Israel" and with the realities of European culture, "such as it is," today? [15]

---

[15] Sean Lucy, in his recent study *T. S. Eliot and the Idea of Tradition* (London: Cohen & West, 1960), approves Eliot's emphasis on the role of Christianity in the formation of European culture, but deprecates Eliot's "insistence on Graeco-Roman culture." That culture, Lucy argues, "played a major part in the spread of Christianity through Europe, but it was a disintegrating Empire, and it is also doubtful whether the cultural principles of its manners, its learning, its philosophies and its art were really compatible with Christianity at all. Some of the results of the so-called 'secularisation of thought' which was part of the Renaissance should certainly make us hesitate to accept an easy formula of 'Greece, Rome, and Christianity' " (6–7). This severely supernaturalist argument flies clean against a long tradition of Christian thought reaching back through Newman to the Greek Fathers. Moreover, he misstates Eliot's and Newman's point in "Greece, Rome, and

Eliot's contention that European culture is an organic unity derived from diverse roots in classical culture and in Israel is not, of course, new or original with him. In the nineteenth century Newman considered the problem, largely in the *educational* terms (the preservation of classical studies) in which Eliot poses it; and while Newman speaks of the uniqueness and power of European civilization with a confidence which no one of our generation would care to imitate, his conclusions are strikingly similar to Eliot's. But he, too, was reduced, in his defense of the unique place of the classics in education, to hints that there is a providential sanction attaching to the methods of intellectual develop-ment contained in the seven liberal arts, and that the deposit of classical culture is "the soil out of which Christianity grew." [16] And Newman speaks very much in Eliot's manner on the joining of the two traditions,

---

Christianity"; instead, both of the latter would say, Greece, Rome, and Israel: the Christian faith would then be the soul of a new and integrated culture such as we know it in mediaeval and modern times. Lucy also rather obscurely berates Eliot for overstressing, in his literary criticism, the role of the classics in the European literary tradition and for neglecting the influence of Christianity. But we have seen Eliot repeatedly speaking of "the necessity of Christianity for the true persistence" of our literary tradition. Lucy claims that Eliot "never speaks directly of the necessity of Christianity" when arguing for the preservation of the classical languages to help maintain the European literary tradition (25); but as we saw above, Eliot insists that "the fundamental defence of Latin and Greek" lies in their association with "the historical Christian Faith" (*SE*, 514). Lucy ends by chiding Eliot: "he could have made a much wider assertion concerning the loss of traditional values which result . . . from the break with our Christian past" (27); one can only protest that nothing could be less equivocal than Eliot's statement that "If Christianity goes, the whole of our culture goes" (*NDC*, 122). On the other hand, Lucy may be correct when he says that "Eliot seems unwilling to state any clear hypothesis" concerning Christianity and the western literary tradition (90).

[16] John Henry Newman, *The Idea of a University*, ed. Charles Frederick Harrold (New York: Longmans, Green and Co., 1947), pp. 224 ff., 228. The whole of Newman's classic lecture "Christianity and Letters" deserves the closest attention in the present context, especially in its implication of a Providential link between the development of the western tradition of natural reason and the growth and history of Christianity, and in its suggestion of "certain analogies" between "Civilization" and Christianity.

though with very little additional help on the precise nature of that marriage:

> Jerusalem is the fountain head of religious knowledge, as Athens is of secular. . . . Each by itself pursues its career and fulfils its mission; neither of them recognizes, nor is recognized by the other. At length the Temple of Jerusalem is rooted up by the armies of Titus, and the effete schools of Athens are stifled by the edict of Justinian. . . . Each leaves an heir and successor in the West, and that heir and successor is one and the same. The grace stored in Jerusalem, and the gifts which radiate from Athens, are made over and concentrated in Rome. This is true as a matter of history. Rome has inherited both sacred and profane learning; she has perpetuated and dispensed the traditions of Moses and David in the supernatural order, and of Homer and Aristotle in the natural. To separate these distinct teachings, human and divine, which meet in Rome, is to retrograde; it is to rebuild the Jewish Temple and to plant anew the groves of Academus.[17]

Again, the essentially *historical* assertion. But in the changed and even disastrous conditions of the twentieth century, the question must be put in more ultimately theological terms: What is the relation of the survival of classical studies to the survival of a European and Christian culture, in the light of the relation of nature and grace? Newman himself begs off, at the end of his lecture on "Christianity and Letters," saying, "To show how sacred learning and profane are dependent on each other, correlative and mutually complementary, how faith operates by means of reason, and reason is directed by faith, is really the subject of a distinct lecture."[18] This intriguing remark hints at a possible direction in filling out the relationship, but neither he nor Eliot follows it up.

For clarification of Eliot's views, we must turn instead to some of his pronouncements in other areas. Much of his inability to define the precise relation between Christianity and classical culture may spring from his general view of the relation of religion and culture. Legiti-

[17] *Idea*, p. 231.
[18] *Ibid.*, p. 231.

mately using "culture" in the modern sociological sense as, in Christopher Dawson's words, "a way of life common to a particular people and based on a social tradition which is embodied in its institutions, its literature and its art" instead of in the older Arnoldian literary sense,[19] Eliot deplores our customary distinction between religion and culture. Beginning with the acceptable proposition that "The development of culture and the development of religion, in a society uninfluenced from without, cannot be clearly isolated from each other" (NDC, 28), Eliot ends with the highly tendentious observation that "bishops are a part of English culture, and horses and dogs are a part of English religion" (NDC, 32). He defends the indissolubility by discussing the crucial fact of the penetration of pagan culture by Christianity:

What perhaps influences us towards treating religion and culture as two different things is the history of the penetration of Graeco-Roman culture by the Christian Faith . . . But the culture with which primitive Christianity came into contact . . . was itself a religious culture in decline. So, while we believe that the same religion may inform a variety of cultures, we may ask whether any culture could come into being, or maintain itself, without a religious basis. We may go further and ask whether what we call the culture, and what we call the religion, of a people are not different aspects of the same thing: the culture being, essentially, the incarnation (so to speak) of the religion of a people. (NDC, 28).

Dawson comments that Eliot's rejection of a *relation* between religion and culture springs from his "ignoring the necessary transcendence of the religious factor," since "the higher religions, and especially Christianity, involve a certain dualism from the nature of their spiritual claims. Here the relation of religion and culture is simply the social corollary of the relation between *Faith* and *Life*."[20] This irreducible

---

[19] See Christopher Dawson, *The Month*, n.s. I (March, 1949), 151–152.

[20] *Ibid.*, p. 155. Eliot's analysis of modern civilization is clearly indebted, however (as he acknowledges in the prefaces to *The Idea of a Christian Society* and *Notes towards the Definition of Culture*), to such Roman Catholic thinkers as Dawson and Jacques Maritain, and to the Anglican Canon, V. A. Demant.

dualism, rejected by Eliot, may be the ultimate explanation of the difficulty involved in making clear how, *historically,* Western civilization was the product of two radically different cultural roots"—the one Graeco-Roman, the other Judaeo-Christian.[21] This fact may also explain a certain ultimate opacity in the question of why the future of classical studies *is* somehow involved in the future of Christian education and formation. Eliot attempts to obviate this opacity by *asserting* a congruence and even identity in status of the two realities (on the analogy of the identity of culture and religion), which in fact remain in themselves distinct.

Eliot's immanentist theory of culture is directly tied to his view of the Church; for him, the Catholic Church, as he defines it, is the historic and enduring embodiment of his asserted unity of religion and culture. As he put it in 1933:

> I believe that the Catholic Church, with its inheritance from Israel and from Greece, is still, as it always has been, the great repository of wisdom. Wisdom seems to be a commodity less and less available in educational institutions. . . . And human wisdom . . . cannot be separated from divine

[21] See William G. Pollard, "Dark Age and Renaissance in the Twentieth Century," *The Christian Idea of Education,* ed. Edmund Fuller (2nd ed.; New Haven: Yale University Press, 1960), p. 3. See also, in the same volume, Reinhold Niebuhr's valuable study, "The Two Sources of Western Culture," pp. 237–254. He insists that "The Christian Faith is primarily Hebraic and does not simply compound Hebraic and Hellenic viewpoints" (243), even though western *culture* is "unique in human history in that it draws upon two different sources for its conceptions of meaning, the Hebraic and the Hellenic" (238). He says that the Greeks were "not predominantly naturalistic," since "they were more interested in the ultimate issues of meaning than in the analysis of efficient cause" (238). Moreover, we did not derive our science from the Greeks and our religion from the Hebrews, since Greek metaphysics was combined with a strong religious impulse; and our ethical heritage unites Greek and Hebraic elements (238–239). Instead, "every conception of meaning which depends upon structure, plan, or scheme is Greek in origin," while all dimensions of meaning which transcend rational and intelligible necessity (freedom, the person, sin, grace) "are derived from Hebrew sources" (239). Eliot of course, with his narrower literary preoccupations, does not see the Greek inheritance in this widened and complex context.

wisdom without tending to become merely worldly wisdom, as vain as folly itself. (*EAM*, 117) [22]

This is "the way of orthodoxy" (*EAM* 135); and Eliot's use of the term, in close conjunction with the dichotomy of classical and romantic, has opened him to the severest strictures. Despite his attempts in 1923 to remove the term "classicism" from the arena of ideological politics,[23] in the same year he accepted the opposition of terms in decidedly polemical fashion, and associated it with his religious views. The difference between classical and romantic, Eliot says, "seems to me rather the difference between the complete and the fragmentary, the adult and the immature, the orderly and the chaotic." Concerning Middleton Murry's dictum that "Catholicism stands for the principle of unquestioned spiritual authority outside the individual; that is also the principle of Classicism in literature," Eliot replies: "Within the orbit within which Mr. Murry's discussion moves, this seems to me an unimpeachable definition, though it is of course not all that there is to be said about either Catholicism or Classicism" (*SE*, 26). Again, in the Dante essay of 1929, the term "antiromantic" is used in a literary discussion to mean both "practical" and "Catholic" (*SE*, 295).[24]

---

[22] J. M. Cameron, in Braybrooke, *A Symposium*, pp. 145–146, sees the root of Eliot's failings as a political thinker in his view of the Church. Cameron correctly notes that the influence of Maurras in *After Strange Gods* was "no more than an episode" in Eliot's development, that the Maurrasien note is scarcely struck thereafter, and that each of Eliot's sociological works is an improvement on its predecessor. But the episode is significant nevertheless, as indicating Eliot's tendency "to neglect what may be called the transcendence of the Church and to overemphasize the immanence of the Church; as did the late Hilaire Belloc in *Europe and the Faith.*"

[23] *The Dial*, LXXV (November 23, 1923), 482.

[24] It seems likely that Eliot's discussion of these terms in the twenties was influenced by T. E. Hulme's remarks, collected and published some years after his death in *Speculations* (1924). Hulme was well aware of the political overtones of the labels "romanticism" and "classicism," the latter especially among the group connected with *L'Action Francaise*, by which Eliot himself was for a time beguiled (Harvest Books ed.; New York, Harcourt, Brace and Co., n.d., pp. 114–115). Hulme also defines classicism and romanticism in large anthropological

These hints were developed at greater length in *After Strange Gods* (1934), where he begins with a highly anthropological definition of tradition as involving "all those habitual actions, habits and customs, from the most significant religious rite to our conventional way of greeting a stranger, which represent the blood kinship of 'the same people living in the same place'" (*ASG*, 18), and broadens it to cover both literary classicism and religious orthodoxy. He notes that "The relation between tradition and orthodoxy in the past is evident enough" (*ASG*, 22), and that the contrast of heresy and orthodoxy "has some analogy to the more usual one of romanticism and classicism" (*ASG*, 26). To be sure, he warns the reader against identifying classicism and Catholicism too far: the connection may not be objective, and may hold only as a personal synthesis (*ASG*, 28). He elaborates the distinction between tradition and orthodoxy this way:

> I hold . . . that *tradition* is rather a way of feeling and acting which characterises a group throughout generations; and that it must largely be . . . unconscious; whereas the maintenance of *orthodoxy* is a matter which which [*sic*] calls for the exercise of all our conscious intelligence. The two will therefore considerably complement each other. . . . And while tradition, being a matter of good habits, is necessarily real only in a social group, orthodoxy exists whether realised in anyone's thought or not. . . . The concepts of *romantic* and *classic* are both more limited in scope and less definite in meaning. (*ASG*, 31–32)

The careful distinctions should be clear enough seriously to qualify Hyman's charge that "order" and "tradition" later *became* "orthodoxy" and that "disorder" later *became* "heresy," [25] and Wellek's flat statement

---

terms, stressing "limit," "tradition," and "discipline" as the heart of the former (116, 117, 120) and associating romanticism with emotional "sloppiness" and drugged consciousness (126, 127). Finally, Hulme argues (117) that "the Church has always taken the classical view since the defeat of the Pelagian heresy and the adoption of the sane classical dogma of original sin." On this whole topic, see Lucy, *T. S. Eliot and the Idea of Tradition*, pp. 33–35.

[25] Stanley Edgar Hyman, *The Armed Vision: A Study in the Methods of Modern Literary Criticism* (2nd ed.; New York, 1955), pp. 63, 66.

that Eliot *"identifies* the classical tradition with the Christian tradition and specifically with the Roman and Catholic tradition which is also politically authoritarian,"[26] especially since statements concerning direct analogies between religious and cultural categories are even harder to find in Eliot after 1933. And yet one can hardly dispute that in Eliot's writings certain literary, sociological, and theological ideas tend to aggregate and shade off into one another without these careful discriminations. The ideas implicit in such terms as classicism, order, civilization, tradition, orthodoxy, Catholicism, and the idea of a Christian society are constantly played off against a cluster of terms including romanticism, disorder, barbarism, individualism, heterodoxy, heresy, "Liberalism, Progress, and Modern Civilization." And even in *After Strange Gods,* where the distinction between tradition and orthodoxy is made with some care, the two terms tend to collapse into one another as part of Eliot's overarching thesis that "the struggle of our time [is] to concentrate, not to dissipate; to renew our association with traditional wisdom; to re-establish a vital connexion between the individual and the race; the struggle, in a word, against Liberalism" (*ASG,* 53).

This is, then, the "age of unsettled beliefs and enfeebled tradition" (*ASG,* 57) which Eliot is in great part rejecting; and belief and tradition are as firmly, if obscurely, linked as ever in his thought. Part of the difficulty is Eliot's broadly anthropological view of "tradition" in *After Strange Gods,* a tradition which, rather perplexingly, also involved the classical tradition. Where, once again, do classical studies and the values inherited from classical culture fit into the broad idea of tradition, which is, historically, closely related to Christian orthodoxy? Eliot himself, in another context, has suggested the complex status of classical values within Christian culture, but has nowhere acknowledged how seriously their autonomy (which he acknowledges) undermines his exaggerated thesis of the virtual identity of Christian and classical values within the synthesis of western culture. I am speaking of Eliot's

[26] Wellek, "The Criticism of T. S. Eliot," p. 430. (Emphasis added.)

discussion, in the late twenties, of the humanism of Irving Babbitt and his followers, one of Eliot's finest and most illuminating performances. "Pure Humanism," as Eliot defines it, would seem to be the permanently valuable *content* of the heritage of classical and humane culture; and Eliot is at considerable pains to preserve the genuine autonomy of these values while still insisting that they cannot be the heart of a culture, that they are in fact "ancillary" to religion. Against Babbitt, Eliot wrote in 1928:

> Humanism and religion are thus, as historical facts, by no means parallel; humanism has been sporadic, but Christianity continuous. It is quite irrelevant to conjecture the possible development of the European races without Christianity—to imagine, that is, a tradition of humanism equivalent to the actual tradition of Christianity. . . .
>
> Humanism is either an alternative to religion, or it is ancillary to it. To my mind, it always flourishes most when religion has been strong. (*SE*, 473, 475)

An antireligious humanism, in Eliot's view, would be "purely destructive for it has never found anything to replace what it destroyed" (*SE*, 475). Concerning Babbitt's "act of faith," presumably in "civilization," Eliot remarks, if by civilization "you mean spiritual and intellectual coordination on a high level, then it is doubtful whether civilization can endure without religion, and religion without a church" (*SE*, 479). It is doubtful, because Babbitt's own followers collapse either "into humanitarianism thinly disguised" or "into a Catholicism *without* the element of humanism and criticism, which would be a Catholicism of despair" (*SE*, 479). Eliot's conclusion is that "the humanistic point of view is auxiliary to and dependent upon the religious point of view. For us, religion is Christianity; and Christianity implies, I think, the conception of the Church" (*SE*, 480). These remarks still imply a harmony between Christian and humanistic values, and an easy dependency of the latter upon the former, which experience suggests is overly optimistic; but by reversing the unacceptable phrase, "a Catholicism

without the element of humanism and criticism," we have a formula—
Christianity *with* the element of humanism and criticism—which, I
think, more adequately than any other passage in Eliot's writings
expresses both the historical and the philosophical relations between the
two ideas. (By "Catholicism," of course, Eliot makes clear (*SE*, 480)
that he does not mean the Roman Catholic Church in an exclusive
sense.) We have the idea of distinction of essence with the possibility of
fruitful union, and the historical image of a stormy and frequently
endangered marriage.

In the following year, in "Second Thoughts about Humanism," Eliot
tried to spell out the precise validity of humanism within the Christian
synthesis and some of its positive and perennial content. He avows that
"I have rejected nothing that seems to me positive" in Babbitt's teaching, and acknowledges that humanism "can be—and is already—of immense value" (*SE*, 481). He sees the humanists' dilemma to lie in their
admitting in one context that "in the past Humanism has been allied
with religion," but in another declaring their "faith that it can in the
future afford to ignore positive religion" (*SE*, 482). He sees Norman
Foerster's literary humanism as an assertion "that there is a 'pure
Humanism' which is *incompatible* with religious faith" (*SE*, 484). Eliot
objects that the humanist system of morals "exists . . . only by illicit
relations with either psychology or religion or both," and that by sharply
separating the "human" from the "natural" the humanist makes use of
the "supernatural" which he denies:

For I am convinced that if this "supernatural" is suppressed, . . . the
dualism of man and nature collapses at once. . . . If you remove from the
word "human" all that the belief in the supernatural has given to man, you
can view him finally as no more than an extremely clever, adaptable, and
mischievous little animal. (*SE*, 485)

Eliot further objects that Foerster's "culture," heavily indebted to
Matthew Arnold, is likely to end in mere *respectability* and the result is

a "pretty thin soup": "Culture, after all, is not enough, even though nothing is enough without culture" (*SE*, 487). Thus does Eliot articulate the precise status of humanistic culture within the larger context of human values. And he ends by insisting that "rational assent" and "intellectual conviction" should precede putting "the sentiments in order"; "intellectual freedom is earlier and easier than complete spiritual freedom" (*SE*, 491). These remarks, which bear the authentic tone of the personal experience of conversion, lead finally to the hopeful view that "There is no opposition between the religious and the *pure* humanistic attitude: they are necessary to each other" (*SE*, 491).

In the course of his agument, Eliot presents a number of functions of "true Humanism" as against the *impure* variety advanced by Foerster. We may select the most important points:

I. The function of humanism is not to provide dogmas, or philosophical theories. Humanism, because it is general culture . . . is concerned less with "reason" than with common sense. . . .

II. Humanism makes for breadth, tolerance, equilibrium and sanity. It operates against fanaticism. . . .

IV. It is not the business of humanism to refute anything. Its business is to *persuade*, according to its unformulable axioms of culture and good sense; . . . it operates by taste, by sensibility trained by culture. It is critical rather than constructive. . . .

V. Humanism can have no positive theories about philosophy or theology. All it can ask, in the most tolerant spirit, is: Is this particular philosophy or religion civilized or is it not?

VI. There is a type of person whom we call the Humanist, for whom humanism is enough. This type is valuable.

VII. Humanism is valuable (a) by itself, in the "pure humanist," who will not set up humanism as a substitute for philosophy and religion, and (b) as a mediating and corrective ingredient in a positive civilization founded on definite belief.

VIII. Humanism, finally, is valid for a very small minority of *individuals*. But it is culture, not any subscription to a common programme or platform, which binds these individuals together. . . . (*SE*, 488–89)

Now these points coincide remarkably with a more recent discussion of "pure" humanism by a French classicist, Fernand Robert, who treats the religious issues involved, however, with an emphasis rather different from Eliot's. Robert, in *L'Humanisme: Essai de Définition,* argues for a revitalized classical humanism of total inclusiveness and rigorous philosophical neutrality, after the pattern of the state schools of France. And yet, though he frankly acknowledges, as Eliot does not, that dogmatic Christians will have difficulties in accepting that strict prohibition against "positive theories about philosophy or theology" which both men prescribe, Robert argues, much in Eliot's manner, that such a humanism need not exclude religion. He seeks a rapprochement with anyone who comes to God out of a realization that "ce qu'il ya de meilleur dans l'homme est divin, donc, par exaltation de ce que l'homme a de plus haut":

> S'il croit . . . que la nature, quelque corrumpue qu'elle soit, peut-être sauvée par des moyens partiellement humains, ou même que l'homme doit coopérer avec Dieu à sa propre salut, il trouvera dans l'humanisme une zone de rencontre avec tous ceux qui pense que l'homme n'a pas besoin de chercher ailleurs qu'en lui-même le moyen de sauver sa propre nature.[27]

Robert also frankly admits, as Eliot does not and, I think, should: "Si l'humanisme n'a rien d'antichrétien, on doit reconnaître qu'il ne suffirait pas à prédisposer à la vie chrétienne." [28] Nonetheless, he ends, as presumably Eliot would, by pointing out the irony involved in that fact that the enemies of the classics in our day are also enemies

[27] Fernand Robert, *L'Humanisme: Essai de Définition* (Paris, Les Belles Lettres, 1946), p. 156.

[28] *Ibid.,* p. 158. Newman saw something of the same point historically. In *The Idea of a University* (p. 89) he frankly admits, on the principle that "the drift and meaning of a branch of knowledge varies with the company in which it is introduced to the student": "Thus the Classics, which in England are the means of refining the taste, have in France subserved the spread of revolutionary and deistical doctrines."

of Christianity, or at least those who concede to Christianity a purely human value, and that such men (refusing to recognize anything above man) somehow fail to recall why a civilization supposed to be Christian maintains itself everywhere by its contact with the greatest spirits of Greek and Latin paganism.[29] But here he stops, as Eliot does, and does not further explicate the relation of classical humanism and Christianity. The virtue of his treatment, however, lies in the assertion of a religiously neutral "pure humanism" which historically *has* had the most intimate relations with Christian civilizations and yet does offer serious difficulties to the dogmatic Christian. In this way he implicitly qualifies Eliot's confident assertion that "there is no opposition between the religious and the *pure* humanistic attitude," while not at all questioning the truth of the statement that "they are necessary to each other" (*SE,* 491).

Eliot is at once too pessimistic and too optimistic to be, perhaps, the ideal exponent of a Christian humanism for our times. In the first place, his adamant refusal to come to terms with "Liberalism, Progress and Modern Civilisation" has consistently blinded him to the possibilities of redeeming modern industrial and technological society.[30] His nearly complete indifference and even hostility toward science and the ways in which it has transformed the modern mind works to invalidate a good deal of his analysis of contemporary civilization. His viewpoint, obviously derived from the traditional "classical humanism" of European schools from the time of the Renaissance onward, is too exclusively literary to do anything approaching justice to the increased complexity of modern life and thought. On the other hand, his analysis of the twin roots of European culture, and of the role of classical studies in the

[29] Robert, *L'Humanisme,* pp. 158–159.
[30] For explorations along these lines, see Walter J. Ong, S.J., *Frontiers in American Catholicism* (New York, Macmillan, 1957), especially the chapter entitled "Technology and New Humanist Frontiers."

maintenance of a Christian tradition, seems far too simple historically and on principle, and paradoxically, despite his somber apocalyptic view of the coming dark ages, it seems too hopeful about the easy relations of Christian faith and natural knowledge in the future. Eliot's limitations extend to much of his poetic output. One must acknowledge the truth of the observations that "The dominant emotions conveyed by the early poems are those of weariness, boredom, frustration, self-doubt and dissatisfaction," [31] and that the early poems up to "Ash Wednesday" are an extended report on the breakdown of communication, the failure to find significance in human relations.[32] And yet surely one must reject the view that *The Waste Land* is a display of Eliot's belief that "the modern world is not important enough to deserve serious treatment" [33] or Hyman's judgment, as the conclusion of his singularly vulgar attempt to "get" Eliot once for all and prove him a fascist and a racist, that the personality which emerges from the poems is "that of a sick, defeated, and suffering man; the discipline and impersonality of the poetry, the 'tradition' of the criticism, chiefly props to sustain him." [34] For Eliot himself seems for a long time to have been aware of his instinct to see all of modern life as "disenchantment and remorse, folly and despair," [35] and the movement of his work, especially the plays, is that of a conscious and painful journey of acceptance of humanity and nature. As early as 1934, in *The Rock,* Eliot had decried "denial of this world" and had counseled, "You must not deny the body" (*CPP,* 107, 111). For behind the prophetic denunciation of the age implied in the early poems was the equally prophetic glimpse of perfection which could at least be apprehended; and the hope for man's future has been increasingly bright in every play since *The Family Reunion.* Only in old age, it seems, however, has Eliot finally left the wasteland and accepted

---

[31] D. S. Savage, in Unger, *T. S. Eliot: A Selected Technique,* p. 143.
[32] See Lucy, *T. S. Eliot and the Idea of Tradition,* p. 143.
[33] See F. Nuhn, in Unger, *T. S. Eliot: A Selected Technique,* p. 133.
[34] Hyman, *The Armed Vision,* p. 91.
[35] Nuhn, in Unger, *T. S. Eliot: A Selected Technique,* p. 136.

a human relationship which of itself gives life meaning, in a play which commits itself to moral choice and makes its key word Love.[36]

Perhaps Eliot's greatest personal contribution to literary humanism in our time is his sense of the crisis of linguistic values in western civilization. His effort has ever been to validate the full power of language, with the total weight of history behind it, as the essence of interpersonal values and as the mainstay of civilization. The critic who in 1921 had written,

> it appears likely that poets in our civilization ... must be *difficult*. Our civilization comprehends great variety and complexity, and this variety and complexity, playing upon a refined sensibility, must produce various and complex results. The poet must become more and more comprehensive, more allusive, more indirect, in order to force, to dislocate if necessary, language into his meaning. (*SE*, 289)

was also the poet who wrote, "And I must borrow every changing shape/ To find expression" (*CPP*, 11) and who put in Sweeney's mouth the words: "I gotta use words when I talk to you/But if you understand or if you dont/That's nothing to me and nothing to you/We all gotta do what we gotta do" (*CPP*, 84). In the choruses from *The Rock* Eliot began those elaborate plays on *speech*, *word*, and *the Word* which were to run through the *Four Quartets*, a poem centrally concerned with "the intolerable wrestle/With words and meanings" and with the knowledge that every new "raid on the inarticulate" is a "fight to recover what has been lost/And found and lost again and again" (*CPP*, 125, 128). But Eliot, the civilized poet seeking to establish "An easy commerce of the old and the new" and declaring that "speech impelled us/To purify the dialect of the tribe/And urge the mind to aftersight and foresight" (*CPP*, 144, 141), is also the Christian poet aware of the limitations of

---

[36] See Gerald Weales, review of *The Elder Statesman*, *The Kenyon Review*, XXI (1959), 477; and Denis Donoghue, *The Third Voice: Modern British and American Verse Drama* (Princeton, New Jersey, Princeton University Press, 1959), p. 163.

humanist scholarship (the inordinate promise of "the wisdom of age" held out by "the quiet-voiced elders") and aware that "Words, after speech, reach/Into the silence" (*CPP*, 125, 121). This is, perhaps, what is "unspeakable,/Untranslatable" in Harry's realization of the "stain" of guilt in *The Family Reunion* (*CPP*, 235), and the silence which Celia sees as necessary in *The Cocktail Party* (*CPP*, 360). Even the richest linguistic inheritance at the center of our culture falls short of expressing all for the Christian poet. And finally, in *The Elder Statesman*, the fact of love bursts through the limits of language: as Charles says,

> Oh my dear,
> I love you to the limits of speech, and beyond.
> It's strange that words are so inadequate.
> Yet, like the asthmatic struggling for breath,
> So the lover must struggle for words.[37]

For Eliot, *history* and *words* and *redemption* are inextricably bound up in one another: "Every phrase and every sentence is an end and a beginning,/Every poem an epitaph. . . ./A people without history/Is not redeemed from time, for history is the pattern of timeless moments" (*CPP*, 144).

It is, then, in the poetry that Eliot convinces us of the ultimate importance of classical linguistic values in his integral Christian vision and task. George Steiner has recently written of "the great crisis of human literacy" in our time, a subject to which we have seen Eliot devote himself, and Steiner sets the problem in much the same context as Eliot does: "The primacy of the word, of that which can be spoken and communicated in discourse, is characteristic of the Greek and Judaic genius and carried over into Christianity. The classic and the Christian sense of the world strive to order reality within the governance of language."[38] As Steiner puts it, "until the seventeenth century the

---

[37] T. S. Eliot, *The Elder Statesman* (London, 1949), p. 107.
[38] George Steiner, "The Retreat from the Word," *The Kenyon Review*, XXIII (1961), 189.

sphere of language encompassed nearly the whole of experience and
reality; today it comprises a narrower domain. The world of words
has shrunk"—through "the submission of successively larger areas of
knowledge to the modes and proceedings of mathematics." [39] Modern
philosophy, art, and music—all are drawn by "the mirage of mathemati-
cal exactitude and predictability." [40] The contemporary writer is reduced
to simpler and fewer words than were Shakespeare and Milton, for
whom words were in natural control of life, both because of the reduced
literacy of a mass culture and because there has been a sharp reduction
in the total of reality which words can adequately control.[41] This
"retreat from vitality and precision" in language is of course parallel to
Eliot's meditation on language as "shabby equipment always deteriorat-
ing/In the general mess of imprecision of feeling,/Undisciplined squads
of emotion"(*CPP,* 128). And even in the face of the cruel fact that most
knowledge is for the future doomed to fragmentation, Steiner nevertheless insists that "we should not readily accede to it in history, ethics,
economics or the analysis and formulation of social and political conduct." [42] He closes by quoting the lines from the *Pervigilium Veneris,*
a poem written "in a darkening time, amid the breakdown of classical
literacy":

> perdidi musam tacendo, nec me Apollo respicit;
> sic Amyclas, cum taceret, perdidit silentium;

" 'To perish by silence': that civilization on which Apollo looks no
more shall not long endure." [43] Here we have the cluster of concerns
which unify Eliot's lifelong labors as critic and poet: the vision of the
end of a civilization, the breakdown of verbal precision, the loss of
human tradition and its values. Confronted by that vision of fearful and

[39] *Ibid.,* pp. 203, 191.
[40] *Ibid.,* pp. 196–202.
[41] *Ibid.,* p. 204.
[42] *Ibid.,* p. 215.
[43] *Ibid.,* p. 216.

perhaps irreversible loss, Eliot has unflinchingly asserted the relevance, the necessity, of the highest standards of classical literacy—the sense of discourse, rhetoric, and poetics—and the qualities of mind ("humanism and criticism") which high literacy has implied in the West, as part of the very essence of the Christian tradition which he has set himself to define, defend, and extend.

Eliot's limitations as an exponent of classical culture, in breadth and depth, are evident enough, though Wellek may overstate the case when he says that for Eliot "The classics are just the wellspring of tradition." [44] And one must regret that about a poet who is personally steeped in classical material and whose own poetry is in innumerable ways indebted to classical examples, we must agree with W. F. J. Knight's statement concerning Eliot's theory of poetic tradition:

I do not know of any passage in which he has discussed the Greek and Latin classics at length as a special part or phrase in this living and massive totality. . . . Eliot clearly enough says that the classics are useful to writers in general and readers in general. . . . But he does not say specifically that the classics are useful to poets as poets; or at least I remember no general argument to show why the later European poets have needed to use so much classical material.[45]

But of his own poetry, as Knight says, there can be no doubt:

he accepts the classical contour. His poems are things made, things meant to exist by themselves. That is, they are not merely jotted messages, handing on, for information, anything in immediate experience happening to be noticed, however sure, however profound. The classical poets must find and use, and use in harmony together and in transmissive growth, their form.[46]

And the whole of that poetry has been read as a plea for classical studies

[44] Wellek, "The Criticism of T. S. Eliot," p. 430.

[45] Knight, "T. S. Eliot as a Classical Scholar," in Braybrooke, *A Symposium*, pp. 121–122.

[46] *Ibid.*, p. 128.

in education at large and in the poet's education in particular.[47] It is this
attempt to keep open the widest channels of communication that makes
Eliot ultimately not merely a Christian spokesman, but that almost
unique combination in our times, a poet of purified religious vision
whose grasp of man's historic situation is nearly unparalleled among
artists in the twentieth century. This theme provides the unity of his
poetic and prose writings, as it does ultimately of the Christian and
classical elements in his thought. The precise tone of that Christian
humanism at its best is caught with exemplary precision in a passage
where Eliot's religious zeal ("any programme that a Catholic can
envisage must aim at the conversion of the whole world"; *EAM*, 123) is
matched by a realistic grasp of human possibilities, that "classical" and
tolerant humanist sense of limitations which Eliot regards as the
"Catholic philosophy of disillusion" (*SE*, 275):

we have to remember that the Kingdom of Christ on earth will never be
realised, and also that it is always being realised; we must remember that
whatever reform or revolution we carry out, the result will always be a
sordid travesty of what human society should be—though the world is never
left wholly without glory. (*ICS*, 60)

[47] See A. J. Creedy, "Eliot and the Classics," *Orpheus: Rivista di Umanità*
(Catania, Italy), I (1954), 42–58, for an ambitious attempt—a subtle, not wholly
convincing, and nowhere fully developed argument—to relate Eliot's remarks in
the critical writings on the classical and humanist tradition to the specific *use*
of classical sources and analogies in the poetry, an argument which hinges on
the ambiguities inherent in the word "tradition" and the phrase "springs of
[spiritual] life." Creedy sees *The Waste Land*'s theme as "the sterility of any
historical era once divorced from the gushing springs of life," and sees *Four
Quartets*, in its concern with the nature of time, as "directly" concerned with
classical studies (47, 48). This latter proposition is illustrated in detail and
sometimes with unconscious humor; for example, the two epigraphs from
Heraclitus "illustrate Eliot's view of the need to keep living and vigorous touch
with the roots of our race, as well as with the spring of our being. If we
neglect classical studies (The Wisdom of the Ages) or if we ignore God (The
Rock of Ages), we shall perish in an abysmal barbarism" (49–50). More
acceptably, he says that "Only through time is time conquered" means *"inter alia*
that our study of the Classics, rightly directed, can help us to relate our
contemporary selves to the whole of history which is meaningless apart from the
context of eternity. The one thing which does illuminate the whole of history and
biography is love" (50). And so forth.

INDEX

Absalom: 16

Achilles: in *Elpénor*, 146

Admetus: in legend, 19; in "Alcestis," 19

Aeneas: 178

Aeschylus: Arnold on, 160 n., 161 n.; mentioned, 135, 156

Aesthetic Education of Mankind: xiii

Africa: Kazantzakis' Odysseus in, 65

After Strange Gods: 184 n., 185, 186

Ajax: in *Elpénor,* 146

Albérès, René: on Giraudoux's use of legend, 135

Alcestis: as virginal woman, 19; as poet's vision, 19, 20; mentioned, 17, 22, 23. SEE ALSO "Alcestis"

"Alcestis": and preromantic German verse, 18–19; pictoral and dramatic in, 19; negation in, 19; life-death theme of, 19; quoted, 19. SEE ALSO Rilke, Rainer Maria

Alcestis: in *The Cocktail Party,* 145–146

Alcmena: in plays and myth, ix, 140, 141, 142–144 *passim,* 145, 147

Alvarez, A.: on *Homage to Sextus Propertius* metre, 106

Amphitryon: in myth and drama, 140, 141, 144, 147

Amphitryon myth: ix: writers treating, 138–139 and n., 140; universality of, 140–141; egocentric motif of, 140; characters of, as symbols, 140; and moral judgments, 140; dramatic bias applied to, 140–141; addition of characters to, 143; changes in, in plays, 144–145; confusion of identity in, 147; criticism on, 148. SEE ALSO *Amphitryon 38*

Amphitryon 38: source of material of, 135; title of, 138–139, 146; Alcmena in, 141; by acts, 141–144; mockery in, 141, 143, 144, 149; quoted, 142, 143; emphasis in, 142, 146; new characters in, 143; the "couple in," 144; mistaken identity in, 144, 147–148; and *The Cocktail Party,* 145–146; commenters on, 147; in Giraudoux's works, 148–149. SEE ALSO Alcmena; Amphitryon; Giraudoux, Jean; Jupiter

Anatomy of Criticism: 134

Anaxagoras: 156 n.

Anouilh, Jean: reinterpretation of legend by, 134–135, 137; *Antigone* of, 134, 135; Greek plays of, 135; mentioned, 89

Antigone: suffering of, 80

Antigone (Anouilh): 134, 135

Antigone (Cocteau): 135

Apollo: of Nietzsche, 6, 23

—of Rilke: his conception of, 6, 29; function of head of, 13; as unifying force, 16; significance of, in *New Poems,* 16; as external representation, 22; and ancient prototype, 22; point of significance of, 23; as god of order, 27; and order of body, 27; mentioned, x, 15. SEE ALSO "Early Apollo"; "Torso of an Archaic Apollo, The"

Apollinaire, Guillaume: and collage technique, 124

Apology: xii

archaeology: rise of, 33; and Joyce, 34

architecture, modern: classical forms in, viii